Dedication.

"You have taught me since I was young, O God,
   and I still proclaim the wonderful things You have
done.
Now as I grow old and my hair turns gray,
   I ask that You not abandon me, O God.
Allow me to share with the generation to come
   about Your power;
Let me speak about Your strength and wonders
   to all those yet to be born."

– Psalm 71:17-18 (VOICE)

This book is dedicated to "the generation to come" of Christian young men who're determined, by God's grace, and to His glory, to become providers, protectors, hunters, and heroes under His governance.

Lionhearted

Making Young Christian Males
Rowdy Biblical Men

By Doug Giles

Published by White Feather Press. (www.whitefeatherpress.com)
Edited by Karen Walker.
ISBN 978-1-61808-899-4
Printed in the United States of America
Cover design by David Bugnon and mobopolis.com

Table of Contents

About the Art

The art work contained in these pages was painted by yours truly. Some originals, herein, are still available. All of these images are available as Open Edition Prints that can be customized to fit your wall space. We print on museum quality canvas, luster paper, wood and for all you metal-heads, we also print on metal. We use only the best inks in our printing process. To see these pieces and more go to DougGiles.Art.

Foreword

Southwood High School in Shreveport, Louisiana had a gang problem so bad that 23 students were arrested in a two-day period from mass brawls involving large groups of boys and the girls.

And then some lionhearted men showed up.

A group of forty fathers split into six-man shifts to volunteer on campus every single day of classes and the entire atmosphere changed from fear and hatred to what students described as "happy, you can feel it." Real men sacrificing time from their jobs and hobbies to provide a masculine presence on campus, and the results have been so amazing that the program is being duplicated all over the nation.

Masculinity is not only healthy and productive, it is absolutely essential for a free society to survive. Using a warped definition of masculinity and throwing in words like "toxic", leftists and radical feminists have removed an essential ingredient of the American success formula and replaced it with the poison of gender confusion. The out-of-control chaos, violence, and destruction is now painfully evident in every blue city where their poison has taken root.

As fad-following, ear-tickling, wimpy pastors shuffle zombie-like right along with the radical effeminizing of Jesus and the church, there has been a massive vacuum filled by barbarian thugs. Just as fatherless boys often join gangs in their search for masculinity never modeled by the men in their life, young men are flocking in droves to the new self-help charlatans peddling a worldly, thuggish definition of successful manhood that will leave them and their community empty and broken.

There is a much better way. Better for those young men, their wives and kids, and most certainly better for the community. In Lionhearted, Doug Giles lays out great advice for young men to do the hard work and make the tough decisions that will lead them down the road of Biblical manhood and the purpose God has for their lives.

We train thousands of young men and women at Patriot Academy, and I hear the same thing from the girls all the time. Where are the Biblically masculine men? Women are crying out in desperation for men to be like those in Issachar that understand the times and know what to do. These women know we are facing very tough times in the years to come, and they want the men in their lives (fathers, husbands, sons, pastors, co-workers) to be able to draw on a strong foundation to navigate the rough waters ahead.

It isn't complicated, but it also isn't easy. Iron sharpening can be a painful and difficult process, but it refines that dull and useless chunk into a finely tuned weapon and that's the kind of men we need in the next generation.

While this book is intended by Doug as a challenge and instruction to individual young men, I see it as a clarion call to the entire culture to replace the missing ingredient of Biblical masculinity so we can restore the republic to a shining city on the hill. Yes, it is time for young men to step up to the challenge, but it is also time for us older men to stop mincing words and soft pedaling out of fear of giving offense. With the culture crumbling around us, your feelings or me stepping on your toes is nowhere on my list of concerns (and never has been for Doug his entire life!). Feel like it or not young man, the very survival of your Nation depends upon your ability to pick up the sword and the trowel and start rebuilding the walls.

Doug is about to tell you how.

Rick Green
America's Constitution Coach
Founder of Patriot Academy

Preface

Dear Young Christian Male. This book you're about to read is meant to challenge you to your very core. It's intent is not to make you feel warm and fuzzy. Some of the chapters will upset you greatly, especially if you're a dandy who was raised with kid gloves by a helicopter mommy. Indeed, these lessons will make you look inside and deal with your bunkum that you're currently blaming other people for.

That said, in addition to the holy introspection contained herein, this book will also shoot adrenaline into your soul. It'll push you to be a godly risktaker and earth-shaker. A veritable Rebel With A Cause just like the Captain of Our Salvation, the Lord Jesus Christ.

If you want a feel-good book that tickles your ears and morphs you into a little Christian popinjay, this slim tome ain't for you. You should put this book down and walk away from it immediately. However, if, young man, if … your motto is to give God your utmost for His highest, and you wanna live a life worthy of Christ's death, then this book will be grist for your mill.

The purpose herein is to make you a veritable pain-in-backside to el Diablo and all his defeated henchmen. To make Satan wish he'd never messed with you. In order to become such an epic Christian man you need to shore up your brain via the Word of God and get some major Holy Ghost cojones and that, my young brother, is what this punchy read is all about.

My regular readers will recognize some of the content from my previous books in this book. The reason I have utilized some of my prior musings is because I don't know if young Christian males have ever laid eyes on my past pertinent info for burgeoning men. Ergo, I've updated some earlier writings of mine for men and added them to this fresh original content made specifically for young Christian males in this unique book for the boys.

Finally, my wife and I were discussing this new book with several single ladies before I addressed a crowd and an epic event. A young woman, who is currently hoping and scoping for a worthy suitor, said she was going to make any dude who comes near her with amorous intent, read and obey my new book, Lionhearted. To wit I said, "Amen sister. I couldn't agree more." Here's a big FYI to all the young Christian males out there in evangelical la-la-land: serious, beautiful, and bold, Christian young women, are not looking to marry a Christian wuss. They're looking for a provider, protector, hunter, and hero; a veritable Dragonslayer. So, young squab, focus on being that type of righteous and rowdy man, and finding a worthy wife will not be a problem at all.

Doug Giles,
Somewhere in Texas

Chapter 1. If You Get This Wrong, Everything Is Wrong.

The year 2016 saw the publication of one of my best, best-selling books regarding The Effeminization of the American Male.

I must warn you: that book is rougher than grandma's breath. Especially if you're a slack-jawed entitled young male. Good luck with getting through that brutal tome. Oh, by the way, I suggest you put on a cup before reading that spicy read. Anyway ...

Indeed, in that #1 Amazon best-seller, I took my verbal sledgehammer to the ubiquitous male tinkerpots that proliferate America's effete milieu and I did it, ironically, with schoolgirl glee.

And you know what?

It resonated with a stack of Americans and international peeps because we sold oodles and oodles of that 202-page waffle-stomper.

For those who know me, you know I don't like to brag, and I don't like to boast, but I like hot butter on my breakfast toast: that book contains some true gems. I'm talking pure gold.

One of the chapters I really liked that I thought would get minimal accolades because the book's bent was not, specifically, driven towards The Church, but more toward the unwashed masses, was my chapter, which showed irrefutably that Jesus was no wuss according to Matthew's account of Christ's life.

I threw that very Christ-O-Centric chapter into my polemic against the pusillanimous because, I believe, the Church is primarily responsible for the effeminate sorry-sod-sicle, which is postmodern America, principally because a lot of ministers are peddling a soft-focused-bearded-lady version of Jesus that has nada to do with the angry young Dragonslayer who kicked up dust on the mean streets of the Middle East many moons ago.

* Here's an FYI for Pastors and Priests: don't whine about the corruption of culture and the despicable nature of most politicians when you crank out gutless puppets instead of courageous prophets.

So, I threw that chapter in kind of as an "aside", y'know ... just to go on record in a widely read book that I think the Church needs to be churched in regard to its rank, and I mean rank, self-inflicted effeminacy and how dare Christians talk smack about culture and politics when we don't have the masculine moxie the prophets, apostles and Christ Jesus Himself sported in spades.

And you know what?

That quick exposition I penned on the book of Matthew, highlighting the masculine qualities of Christ in contrast to the squealy, effeminate tenor of our current emasculated ecclesiastical emissaries has garnered more unsolicited positive feedback, especially from the "laity", than every other chapter in that *caliente* read.

Can you say, "Yahtzee?" I'm very certain I struck a nerve.

Which brings me to this lesson about Jesus's masculinity.

Masculinity, and "men who would be men", and "testosterone", and "boys just being boys", are being attacked more in this sassy society than a fudge fountain would be at a plus-sized pool party.

Not only is classical masculinity vilified by the mouthy misandrists but the manly qualities of Jesus are getting about as much love from the pulpit as I would if I rocked up, unannounced, to a radical lesbian Marxist goat roast.

Some of you are thinking, "Dude ... what's your point?"

My point is, and I'll prove it in the next few minutes from the book of Matthew, that when it comes to Jesus Christ, as defined by the scripture, He's any- and everything other than a Precious Moments figurine. And for little ol' me, it's the sin of sins to neuter what the scripture screams about that thirty-year-old rebel from Galilee.

For instance …

When the misinformed thinks of Jesus nowadays, one imagines ...

An overly ebullient, grinning hick with a curly mullet, a man bag, and a quaint southern drawl, who spits out more aphorisms than a motivational speaker on crystal-meth-laced Mountain Dew.

Or The Nazarene gets painted as some rambling, Rasputin-like mystic who strings together long, illogical stories like an unshorn, bong hit-inspired, Matthew McConaughey grad speech.

Either that or *Jesus Cristo* gets pitched as some unisexual, religious, gluten-free Gucci model who might confuse us with regard to his actual gender, but he's crystal clear with his message that we should all be tolerant of the ridiculous no matter how much it offends reason.

Two things are for certain in our culture's postmodern paranormal messaging regarding Christ and Christians:

Jesus is not masculine and ... Christianity is for pansies

Indeed, our wussified culture (and that includes the Church) has created for themselves a wussified, Faux Christ, who's nicer than the actual Jesus and has little to nothing to do with the rebellious, young Galilean who jettisoned evil priests, fish-slapped putrid politicians and crushed *el Diablo* two thousand years ago.

Consequently, His followers are expected to produce gelded disciples who do not upset the world like the first-century believers did.

Well, as you can imagine, young man, I'm here to blow that nonsense all to smithereens.

The real Jesus of the scripture was a very hard act to follow.

Jesus was the epitome of a man's man.

Yep, the Jesus of the scripture crushed the serpent, drank and made wine, was a carpenter before Home Depot and power tools, fashioned a whip and turned over the book tables of the religious dandies of His day, bashed false prophets and wicked politicos and sacrificially gave up His life as a ransom for many. To make that Man into some effeminized, skinny hippie with long, pretty hair as far as I'm concerned, is really close to the unpardonable sin.

If you need further proof that I'm not a bubble off level, then grab your journal Queequeg, and check out my observations of the Rowdy Christ from the Book of Matthew.

1. Jesus was a Heroic Savior. He sacrificed His life via a brutal crucifixion for our goofy and abominable sinful condition. That is the epitome of masculinity. Indeed, no self-obsessed quasi-male would go anywhere near that ignoble death on behalf of others, but Christ did, willingly and joyfully (Heb. 12:1-3, Matt. 1:18-21).

2. When Jesus was a toddler, He terrified Satan so much that demon-possessed Herod tried to kill Him before He could become a man and wreck the devil's dream of global domination (Matt.

2:1-6).

3. Jesus defeated Satan's temptations in the Wilderness on a very empty stomach. That's masculine warrior stuff in case you didn't catch that (Matt. 4:1-11).

4. Jesus preached repentance. Turn or burn, baby. He said unless you do a 180 away from your current and corrupt glide path you will not inherit the Kingdom of God. Nobody preaches that anymore, but Christ did because Jesus wasn't an evangelical twinkie (Matt. 4:12-17).

5. Also, please note that Jesus wasn't some fear-laden hamster and He condemned fear in His followers. Did they tell you that at Youth Group (Matt. 6:25-34)?

6. Jesus promised pain in life. Yep, He preached the brutal truth and not pain-free, no conflict, pixie dust. He also said if you build on obedience to His word, you'd successfully ride all storms out. If not, you won't. That's called straight talk, y'all (Matt. 7:24-28). That's how a masculine Savior rolls. Can you dig it?

7. Jesus said, Dear young male Christian, that in this life you'll be called the Devil and people will attempt to kill you. Following Him will bring conflict, even within your own family, and it could ultimately cost you your life. In light of this, He has commanded you not to fear, not to deny Him and His word, and to love Him more

than life itself. That's the fruit Jesus said a true disciple will exhibit (Matt.10:24-39). Once again, pretty pastors don't preach that anymore, but Jesus did.

8. Christ said entrance into the kingdom of Heaven requires spiritual violence. You have to view Him and it as a precious prize that is sought with the most ardent zeal and intense exertion. If you don't believe me, google Matt. 11:12 in the Amplified Classic Edition of the Bible.

9. Jesus didn't obey His mommy all the time. If mommy's desires conflicted with His heavenly Father's will, then mommy got ignored (Matt. 12:46-50). That's dude stuff right there.

10. Jesus didn't tell quaint moralistic fables. His stories were scary tales of damnation to those willfully blind and deaf to His commands. See Matt. 13:10-17 for a blistering masculine example.

11. Jesus didn't play games with hard-hearted goobers who blew off His person and works. He left them in the dust once He realized they were not interested in what He had to say (Matt.13:53-58). Are you getting this yet? Because I'm laying it down pretty thick.

12. When people described Jesus, they didn't say He is such a sweetie. They didn't paint Him as a very likable person. His contemporaries said Jesus was like Elijah, or Jeremiah, or John The Baptist. In other words, young dude, Christ was

about as cuddly as a cactus. Especially if you were on the wrong side of truth (Matt. 16:13-17).

13. Here's another ditty about Jesus that'll run afoul with the airy-fairy, porcelain-skinned pastors that fill pulpits in the oh-so-effete evangelical milieu. Jesus declared that true greatness, in God's eye, has zero to do with wealth and fame, power and position, but is exemplified by sacrificially serving other people. Who the heck says that anymore? If you want to be a biggie big shot, according to God's eternal perspective, then be a slave to others (Matt. 20:17-28).

14. In Matthew 23, sweet Jesus publicly barbequed the most religious clique on this third rock from the sun. Christ pronounced eight woes upon their ilk for irrevocably denying all of His calls to repentance. Once again, that's masculine to the core.

And lastly, after Jesus was abandoned by His disciples and God, beaten beyond recognition, and then crucified and killed. Please note that after He rose from the dead, He did not seek vengeance. He did not pout because nobody liked Him. He did not set fire to a daycare center because of His wounded inner child. No, and indeed, He turned their hate into His love, grace, and forgiveness and He commanded His disciples to spread that Good News all over this terra firma. And young gents … if that ain't masculinity, I don't know what is.

Ergo, my beloved young Christian males, my point in this first lesson, in case you still haven't gotten it, is this:

Lionhearted

Jesus, plain and simple, was the epitome of a man's man. And if you don't understand that by now then I don't have the grace, patience, or crayons to further explain it to you.

If you're using this book in a group setting, here are some questions to throw around, chew on, and discuss. Enjoy.

1. When you imagine Jesus, do you see Him as a nice religious, long-haired moral role model, or a grave-defying Dragonslayer who came to destroy the powers of darkness?

2. Do you think Doug's nuts when he says, "… Our wussified culture (and that includes the Church) has created for themselves a wussified, Faux Christ, who's nicer than the actual Jesus and has little to nothing to do with the rebellious, young Galilean who jettisoned evil politicians and priests and crushed *el Diablo* two thousand years ago?"

   • If you answered "yes," then give your group a few examples of how the culture and the Church have "wussified" Christ and Christianity.

   • Also, why do you think they would do something like make a Jesus who's more pliable than the Christ of the scriptures?

3. After reading Doug's dissection of the Book of Matthew, and the overt masculine traits of Jesus Giles highlighted, did that change how you've been seeing The Son of God?

Chapter 2. The Three Non-negotiables For Biblical Young Men.

"I have written to you, young men, because you are strong, and the word of God remains in you, and you have overcome the evil one."

— 1 John 2:14 (NASB)

I think it's cool that the Apostle John, one of the hand-picked original twelve disciples of The Ultimate Dragonslayer, Christ Jesus Himself, took time to give a shout-out to the young Christian dudes back in the day. Yep, one of the Sons of Thunder (Mark 3:17) gave a big high-five to the fledgling warriors in his midst.

Juan said the young men that he rolled with within Christ's first-century Church weren't weak and pathetic

Christian wussies, who were biblically illiterate and dominated by the superfluity of naughtiness. Nope, John says his young charges were "strong, and the word of God remained in them, and they had overcome the evil one."

Dang, man.

What an honor to have that said about you, eh? Heck, I'm sixty years old at this writing and I'll take that accolade. Can I get a witness from my older brothers?

Again, and wow, John said the juvenile cats that he interfaced with in days of yore were …

Strong.

Full of the word of God.

And had overcome the Devil.

Hoorah, baby! Hoo-rah.

The Amplified Bible, Classic Edition puts it this way, "I write to you, young men, because you are strong and vigorous, and the Word of God is [always] abiding in you (in your hearts), and you have been victorious over the wicked one." – 1 John 2:14.

Let's break this down, shall we?

First off, John said the young men he was familiar with in the Body of Christ were strong and vigorous. A lot of young men today are weak and languorous. Especially Christian young men. If you don't believe me, just check out most of your Christian youth groups from sea to shining sea. The majority of the Church's young ones are feeble, sluggish, weak, delicate, soft, effete, lackadaisical, unhealthy, effeminate, biblically stupid, and wimpy and you know that's true, generally speaking.

Lionhearted

When one thinks of your typical Christian young man the image that's conjured up is not one of a robust, young warrior but instead it's some shallow-chested, skinny-armed, and pencil-necked do-gooder. Or it's an obese, teenage couch-surfing indoor boy who stares at his demonic "Smart Phone" most of the day and has a "kick me" sign on his back. If you think I'm full of specious doo on that assessment, just ask the young single ladies who're hoping and scoping for a sharp and hardy beau within the Church. They'll confirm the dire dearth of legit manly dudes within Christendom.

John was impressed with the young men that made up the Early Church. I'm sure some of you are thinking, "Yeah? So what?" Well, here's why I think John's mad props are of serious importance. John, you see, was no delicate little disciple. The nickname Jesus gave John was "Son of Thunder." John brought the thunder, folks. I wonder, what nickname Jesus would give your typical teenage Christian nowadays? Possibly, "Son of Bieber?" Who knows? Anyway, back to John.

John was a fisherman. Professional fishing is a tough job. John abandoned everything to follow Jesus. Yes, he risked it all for the Son of God. John cast out devils, healed the sick and he was in Christ's inner circle along with his brother James and Peter.

John saw and heard things that would melt most human beings into a warm pile of goo. Oh, and speaking of warm goo, John was boiled in oil and exiled to the Isle of Patmos where he spent his remaining years in prison for his unwavering faith.

John wrote the Book of John, First, Second, and Third John, and The Book of Revelation. John witnessed the brutal death, burial, resurrection, and ascension of The Son of God. In addition, every one of his *compadres* who were selected by Christ were murdered for their faith, sans Judas.

Hence, my beloved, the fact that John was impressed by the young men he was addressing says something because I bet ol' John was a tough man to impress. I wonder if John would be gobsmacked, in a good sense, with Christian young people today? I don't know but I kind of doubt it.

One good way to impress a dude like John and curry favor from Christ is to embody the initial description Johnny Boy gave these young men, namely get strong and vigorous.

Hey, Christian young man... quit being so frail. God didn't create you to be a little daisy. Cease and desist with the listlessness. Stop being indolent. If you don't know what that means, then google it. Be strong in body, mind, and spirit. Do the stuff that makes you sweat and toughens your decrepit backside up. Work out at least four times a week. Study apologetics and the Christian worldview. If the aforementioned seems too tough for you or unappealing then, if I were you, I'd at least start learning Mandarin because you're going to become China's prison chick soon.

Speaking of China, back in the summer of 2021, China officially banned sissy men from Chinese television in order to promote more masculine role models.

Lionhearted

Garsh ... "Why would the Chinese do something like that?" asks the effete evangelical.

Well, I will tell you why, my little darling. China, you see, wants to rule the world and they think in terms of millennia. Therefore, frail Christian, they are gonna need multi-generations of masculine men to pull off their communist machinations of global domination. To accomplish this long-term goal they've decided they need to scrub effeminate men from TV and push more masculine role models as part of their "healthier society".

In addition to that masculine move, the CCP is also limiting the amount of time kids can spend online playing video games to three hours a week and only on the weekends. Succinctly, all androgynous, sleek, girlish, effeminate, K-Pop, he/she's, "What is that?", tinkerpot males that are celebrated in South Korea and Japan don't get to see the light of day in China. Chinese TV put a resolute end to that unnatural and abnormal aesthetic and instead are vigorously promoting masculinity, excellence, traditional Chinese culture, and the revolutionary mindset. Meanwhile, they export to the U.S. the TikTok app that pushes on our young men all the effeminized bunkum they just banned while simultaneously stealing all our data, and brainwashing our kids while spying on the dupes who downloaded their app.

Think about it. China puts a national ban on sissy men and severely restricts gaming for the kiddos while they promote traditional Chinese culture and revolutionary ideology as America celebrates drag queens prancing around the White House, telling us all to get the mystery jab, while RuPaul dons the front cover of a box of Cheez-

Its. We're in deep yogurt folks unless the U.S.A., and the Church in particular, doubles down and starts promoting traditional and godly masculinity.

The Devil loves delicate and wimpy young men. Especially if they're "Christians." So do political control freaks. So do all our foreign enemies. Therefore, young squire, make certain you don't assist the aforementioned axis of evil by being a tepid, weak, and wheezing young toad.

Here's some practical tips to make you a strong and vigorous Christian.

- Work out hard, 30-60 minutes a day, at least four times a week. I've been doing that for the last forty-six years.
- Begin training jiu-jitsu or some other form of martial arts.
- Get some sun, indoor boy.
- Get punched in the face. More about that later.
- Walk with your chest out and head up and not like some iPostured dipstick staring at your soul-sucking "smartphone" all the time.
- Also, pick up the pace when you walk and not like most young men who move like a manatee swimming in lukewarm sludge in the intensified gravity of the planet Jupiter.
- In addition, quit sitting for long periods of time unless of course your dream is to become an obese, high blood pressure, ticking time bomb with diabetes and soaring cholesterol before you turn thirty.

Lionhearted

Please note, once again, young man, that the Holy Spirit, via the Apostle John, praised the Christian young men for being strong and vigorous. Can your mommy or your daddy or your hipster youth pastor say that about you? If not, get busy rectifying your inglorious condition. This is an easy fix. It's all about discipline. By the way, the world belongs to the disciplined. Therefore, glorify God in your mortal body by being strong and vigorous versus being weak and languorous (1Cor. 6:20; 1Tim. 4:8).

Another awesome accolade John gave the young men was that the Word of God was always abiding in their hearts. These young men had a high view of scripture and they dined on it regularly.

Young warrior: If you wanna tick off el Diablo and his woke masses, and truly please The Rock of Our Salvation I'd do the following …

Number One. Read a physical, not digital, Bible in public. That'll make anti-theistic snowflakes' heads explode. Plus, it'll encourage other young Christians, who're ashamed of the Word of God, to cowboy up and read it in public as well. In addition, some holy and hot girl might see that you don't care who sees you read the Bible in public because you love God too much to fear men and she'll want to marry you and have 15 kids with you. Or something like that.

Number Two. Read the Bible all the time. The powers of darkness are going to assault you constantly so you should be in the Word of God constantly. Duh. Become an expert swordsman with the scripture. Memorize it. Meditate upon it. Learn that book from front to back, from Genesis to Revelation, and from soup to nuts. Don't be a casual Christian with the Word of God. That's disgusting. That's what tinkerpots do. Oh, by the way, Christ said the half-baked Christians make him wanna vomit (Rev. 3:16). So don't dilly-dally regarding knowing the Scripture. Go all in. Master it.

Number Three. Read, pray, and meditate in the Word of God at least thirty minutes a day. Some young clown is thinking, "Man, that's a lot. I don't have time to do that." Yes, you do. What your flesh and/or what some demon just told you about "not having enough time" is a lie. You do have the time. If you have time for gaming, porn, endless YouTube videos, and talking to your girlfriend for hours on end, then you have at least thirty minutes a day to renew your mind with the Word of God. So, quit lying to yourself about not having enough time. Make the time and watch God richly bless your life.

Number Four. Focus on getting closer to God when reading the Word. Don't just read to get historical intel and mere head knowledge of the scripture. Demons can do that (James 2:19). The Devil knows the Word of God better than most Christians. The late atheist of note, Christopher Hitchens, who was no fan of God, had a mighty amount of Bible knowledge but that didn't help him at all. When you're in the Verbum Dei, ask The Lord to reveal Himself to you. Ask the Holy Spirit to teach you His way. Ask Him to make His word shape you into a force and not a farce, for His glory.

Number Five. Get a hard copy of the Bible. When I got converted at the ripe old age of twenty-one, I devoured the Scripture. I think I destroyed, through use, four Bibles in three years. One of the Bibles I kept together with duct tape I had beat up its binding so badly. The cool thing about having a physical copy of the Bible versus a mere digital one is you can write in it. I've got some Bibles that look like Hillary Clinton's coloring book after she lost to Trump in 2016. You can barely read the page because of my margin notes. If something flicks your switch, highlight it and/or underline it. If God shoots a promise into your heart via the Word of God, date that bad boy and claim it, and watch God bring it to pass. Feel free to use and abuse that Bible for His glory. If you're not thrashing your Bible, then it's probably not doing you any good. Wear it out and then leave it for your kids and grandkids to have after you croak.

Number Six. Let the Word of God shape your view of family, Church, culture, and politics. Crass cultural icons and big government goons hate having the Word of God butt into their plans for satanic domination. Wherefore, young squire, let the scripture sculpt how you view the world and not some devil-worshiping, flesh-loving, vapid dork in DC and/or Hollywood.

So, what do we have, heretofore, my young brothers? Well, John said the young men he knew in the Church were strong and vigorous and the Word of God was always abiding in their hearts. Those first two accolades set the stage for the last whopping kudos John gave to the young dudes namely, "You have been victorious over the evil one." Wow! Just, wow. Young men overcoming the Devil? You don't hear that too much in most youth groups. It's always hearing young men complain about getting their butt handed to them by the Devil and not vice versa. John said his crew of young Turks throttled the ancient Serpent.

Check it out…

- Compromise wasn't ruling their life.
- Political correctness wasn't dominating them.
- They weren't duped by lying spirits.
- They weren't lured from the straight and narrow by demonic appeals to pride and autonomy.
- They were not hamstrung by a deep porn addiction.
- They were not dazzled by the fleshy delights of Rome.
- They didn't stay a perpetual "woe is me" victim of self-pity.
- They were not buffaloed by the bad theology and the shady politics of their day.

Whatever Satan threw at these young men they crushed out of their lives and were victorious over Satan's various demonic devices. Can you say, "#boom!"

---

1. How many Christian "influencers" have you seen challenging the Church to man up in body and in mind, and in habits? Have you seen very opinionated and preachy three-chinned Crisco-sweating lard balls give dire warnings about

gluttony and sloth?

2. Reality check: Which of these has God's Word been to you and why? (Pick all that apply)

    - A chore to be avoided
    - A moral checklist
    - A collection of stories
    - Training for life
    - Life-giving divine truth

3. Doug said some of his hard-copy Bibles are in worse shape than that fisherman and his dog who spent three months lost at sea... why is that a good thing? How could that make a difference in your life?

4. What would a "no-compromise" life mean to you?

5. If Christian men learned and exercised biblical discipline over their own bodies, minds, and habits — would that change how the world saw/ interacted with them? In what way?

Chapter 3. This Sin Is Currently Crushing Many Young Males.

"Or do you not know that the unrighteous will not inherit the kingdom of God? Do not be deceived; neither fornicators, nor idolaters, nor adulterers, nor effeminate, nor homosexuals, nor thieves, nor the covetous, nor drunkards, nor revilers, nor swindlers, will inherit the kingdom of God."

— 1 Corinthians 6:9,10 (NASB1995)

Dear Young Dude: That passage you just read from 1 Corinthians 6:9-10 can be filed under, "Scriptures you'll never hear preached on in your lame youth group or in your hipster church but there they sit … bigger than Dallas."

The apostle Paul said, by inspiration of the Holy Spirit, that the male who is effeminate will not inherit the kingdom of God. In other words, they're not saved if they do not repent from that particular sin.

Succinctly, effeminacy in males is a perversion of what God intended a man to be and is, therefore, a big whopping no-no. Don't shoot me, folks. I'm just the messenger. I'm just reading what the Word of God says is an abomination. If you wanna get angry about that verse, then I suggest you take it up with God because He's the one who inspired Paul to pen that down for all eternity.

What's interesting, in our oh-so-sassy evangelical milieu, is that the preponderance of the aforementioned vices does get touched when the pastor finally dares to do a message against sin.

However, I cannot remember in my lifetime of sixty-plus years when I've heard a sermon that seared the effeminate male for his effeminacy. Can you recall one message against that transgression? As stated, I cannot, but then again maybe my Prevagen hasn't kicked in hard enough this morning for a total recall of every sermon I've ever heard preached.

Question. Doesn't effeminacy seem out of place in that abysmal list of abominations? It's kinda like in Revelation 21:8 where the coward is grouped up with people who're anti-theistic, abominable, murderers, sexually immoral; that practice black magic, worship idols, and spew lies who end up getting eternally tossed into the lake which burns with fire and brimstone.

Indeed, nowadays, a young man who is effeminate and or cowardly is no big whup. It's almost commonplace and in some sectors of society, it's even celebrated in males. However, according to 1 Corinthians 6:9, it is the trait of the damned and a sin to be repented of. Yep, the Triune Godhead is not cool, at all, with effeminacy in men.

So, what does it mean for a male to be effeminate? What is God condemning as a work of the flesh that's a manifestation of demonic spirits who work in conjunction with our fallen nature (Eph. 2:1-3)?

The Greek word used for the effeminate is *malakos* which means "soft" as is fine clothing that is delicate to the touch; a fabric that's luxurious and dainty (Matt. 11:8; Luke 7:25). Paul obviously did a Holy Spirit-inspired play on words with this unholy vice. Essentially, young man, Paul is saying, if you're a softy, if you're delicate and dainty, then you need to repent of that sin like a fornicator needs to repent of his fornication, you dig? In God's eyes, effeminacy in males is just as foul as the most messed up sins the world heaps scorn upon.

Other meanings for malakos include a male being …

1. Malleable. Easily controlled or influenced.

2. Mild. Moderate in type, degree, effect, or force.

3. Smooth. Free from hair, whiskers, or stubble.

4. Squashy. Flabby, mushy, pulpy, spongy, and squishy

5. Mellow. Suggesting softness or sweetness.

6. Compliant. Yielding; bending; pliant; submissive.

7. Waxen. Weak, pliable, or impressionable.

8. Quaggy. Of the nature of a quagmire; yielding or trembling under the foot, as soft, wet earth; spongy; boggy.

9. Meek. Easily imposed on; submissive.

10. Subdued. Conquered; overpowered; crushed; submissive; mild.

Wow. That's a heckuva mental image, eh?

Here's a FYI, young man...

1. God hasn't called you to be easily controlled or influenced except by Him.

2. God hasn't called you to be mild. He's called you to be wild (Ps. 92:10).

3. God hasn't called you to be a spongy and squishy Christian quagmire but a strong and vigorous devil destroyer (1Jn. 2:14).

4. God hasn't called you to be a little sweetie-pie but salt and light to this dank world (Matt. 5:13-16).

5. God hasn't called you to be a compliant butt-kisser to bad actors and bad ideas, but rather a bold truth-teller (Mark 8:38).

6. God hasn't called you to be submissive to anyone, anywhere at any time unless it is in accordance with His word and that which is holy, just, and good.

7. And lastly, young dude, God definitely has not called you to be conquered, crushed, and overpowered by the Devil. His goal, through you, by the power of the Holy Spirit, is for you, my little brother, to kick maximum demonic backside for the glory of God. Therefore, young Christian, dissuade yourself of any notion that being a little softy is God's will for your life because it is not, and that notion is sinful and demonic.

By the way, the effeminate traits of being soft, malleable, mild, quaggy, squashy, etc., are more of an internal vice than an external problem in our politically correct days of conformity to anti-theistic stupidity. Here's what I mean. I know young men who probably can't bench press their body weight, who still drink from straws and pay eight bucks for a Frappuccino who'll also take you to task if something unholy, unjust, and ungood comes out of your mouth and forms into public policy. They're not a monster on the outside but they are a monster on the inside. Kinda like David, Samson, and Elijah who were not statues of physical perfection but simple men, like you and me, internally powered by the Spirit of The Living God to do holy and awesome masculine stuff.

In contrast to that example, I know young men who're terrifyingly big, physically strong, with skills to kill, literally, who are also internally defeated and unable and unwilling to stand against the enemies of that which is holy, just, and good. So, my question to you is ... which of the twain is exhibiting effeminacy, huh?

Finally, young squire, please note in 1Cor. 6:11 Paul said the males became biblical men and got free from the sin of effeminacy. Check it out ... "Such were (Operative word, "were") some of you; but you were washed (Forgiven and cleansed from the sin of effeminacy), but you were sanctified, but you were justified in the name of the Lord Jesus Christ and in the Spirit of our God."

Our crass culture, Satan, and all our physical enemies, both foreign and domestic, want young Christian males to become wussies and stay wussies, internally and externally. If you're a pliable little male softy, then you're easy for them to control. That's not cool with God. In Christ, He wants you to be a provider, protector, hunter, and hero. God made you to be masculine, not feminine. Ergo, my young brother, revel in the God-inspired testosterone fog. Let His word transform you away from the garbage this world wants you to bow to.

> *"I appeal to you therefore, brethren, and beg of you in view of [all] the mercies of God, to make a decisive dedication of your bodies [presenting all your members and faculties] as a living sacrifice, holy (devoted, consecrated) and well pleasing to God, which is your reasonable (rational, intelligent) service and spiritual worship. Do not be conformed to this world (this age), [fashioned after and adapted to its external, superficial customs], but be transformed (changed) by the [entire] renewal of your mind [by its new ideals and its new attitude], so that you may prove [for yourselves] what is the good and acceptable and perfect will of God, even the thing which is good and acceptable and perfect [in His sight for you]."*

> – Romans 12:1-2 (AMPCE).

Lionhearted

1. How has the sin of effeminacy changed the culture? How has it changed the church?

2. Giles says that effeminate traits of being soft and malleable are "more of an internal vice rather than an external problem." What does he mean by that? Why is it important to note?

3. Doug makes it clear that effeminacy isn't about size and strength. So, what is it about?

4. Give an example of a time someone you know took a bold stand for a righteous cause.

Chapter 4. A Command To Young Men That Gets Ignored By Groovy Youth Pastors.

I got married when I was twenty-five. Soon after our nuptials my wife and I were invited to this fabulous party filled with wealthy and pretty people. At that juncture, my wife and I had very little money. We lived in a house that was a little bigger than a full-size Chevy van. Yep, we did not have much from a materialistic point of view but, OMG baby, we were brimming over with vision and were in earnest about being used by God to put a big ol' jagged scar on Satan's haggard backside.

During the soiree, a very wealthy non-Christian young businessman asked me what my goals were for the future. I told him I wanted to preach the gospel to as many people as I can. He told me, and I quote, "Dude... don't take life so seriously." Then he and his father had a good chuckle at my expense and then moved on feeling very superior to my po' little Christian self.

If I didn't have a stranglehold on the Word of God, I probably would've let that frat boy's critique of my glide path shame me from my holy duties. But alas, the Word of God was dwelling in my heart, and it shot down that bad advice from Richie Rich and it helped keep my young nose to the grindstone, taking life and God seriously.

Here's one of the verses I digested as a young Christian man that assisted me greatly in cudgeling off Satan's temptation to stupidity, frivolity, and a fascination with this world's Vanity Fair of earthly delights. Check it out …

> *"In the same way, urge the young men to behave carefully, taking life seriously."*

> –Titus 2:6 (TLB)

The AMPC puts it this way … "In a similar way, urge the younger men to be self-restrained and to behave prudently [taking life seriously]."

Paul instructed Titus to tell the young men to behave carefully, show self-restraint, behave prudently, and take life seriously.

I believe in order to remedy the particular problems we're facing in the church, family, and state, we need a cool metric ton of young masculine Christian protagonists to lead the way.

So, young Turks, salvaging the planet is on you.

Lionhearted

Awww ... what's that I hear? Are you crying? Do you want your mommy? Should I call the wambulance? Do you need a blankie or are you going to rise to the occasion and be a kingdom player at a young age, huh?

Paul tells Titus to command young men, exhorting them to be sober-minded. Young men are to be free from intoxicating influences. And we're not just talking about booze and dope but worldviews that are demonic. Young squire, you are to be free from pressures to conform to that which is not according to God's will and way.

Herewith are five reasons young men should be sober-minded.

One. God commands you to be, duh. That's not a suggestion, young squire. That's a command. To not be sober-minded is to sin. If you're not sharp, solid, and smart ... ie. sober-minded ... you're sinning. That's what you call not loving God with all your heart, soul, mind, and strength. God commands you in the most urgent manner, to be sober-minded in your youth. Guess what young dude, you get to decide whether or not you will obey that injunction. Go ahead. Ignore it. And let's see what happens to you in the next twenty years.

Two. Why be sober-minded? Well, death and judgment are waiting for young men, not just us old cats. We all must appear before the judgment seat of Christ. I've seen many young men die. Just because you're young it doesn't mean you're invincible. Nothing is promised to you, years-wise. We don't know when we will spring off this mortal coil. The day of your death could be just around the corner. 2 Corinthians 5:10 says, "For we must all (that includes young males) appear before the judgment seat of Christ, so that each one may be recompensed for his deeds in the body, according to what he has done, whether good or bad."

Three. So, young men, why be sober-minded? Well, aside from it's commanded and death and judgment await you and nothing's really promised as far as life-span goes; Another *bueno* reason is this: What you are now, more than likely, you will be later. Young idiots morph into old idiots. Young drunks turn into old drunks. Young perverts become old liver-spotted lecherous men. Yep, barring a true conversion, by the power of the Holy Spirit, you'll just become older and worse. A leopard cannot change its spots (Jer. 13:23). Here's a question for you? Would you like to get on what God's doing now or wait 'til you're 60 and bald and tired? Most young fools say, "I'll get serious about God later. Y'know, after I've sowed some wild oats." But the scripture says today's the day of salvation (2Cor. 6:2). You don't know at all what tomorrow holds (James 4:13,14). Personally, I'm so glad God karate-chopped me when I was young. I'd be dead or in prison if it weren't for a massive clean Holy Ghost break from my young sin-lovin' demonic flesh.

Four. Why should young men be sober-minded? Here's a good reason: 1 Peter 5:8 says, "Be of sober spirit, be on the alert. Your adversary, the devil, prowls around like a roaring lion, seeking someone to devour." If you're goofy and thoughtless the devil will make certain you're road-kill on the Highway to Hell. Here's an FYI to the young males: Satan is here to steal from you, kill you, and destroy you (Jn. 10:10) and he operates by stealth, just like a lion. So, sobriety of spirit is a must, young man. By the way, your typical young man isn't aware of Satan's desire to destroy him forever. If you do not resist him, like Peter said, he'll walk all over you and yours. Again 1 Peter 5:8. Be of sober spirit, be on the alert. Your adversary, the devil, prowls around like a roaring lion, seeking someone to devour.

I've been on three African lion hunts. My male lion charged us, and I dispatched him as he came in close, baring tooth, fang, and claw to permanently part my hair. I will never forget that. When my buddy Glenn was hunting his lioness a few years ago I accompanied him. Our trackers picked up his lion's tracks and off we went on foot following her pugmarks. We'd been tailing her on foot for about three miles when we stopped to chill and drink some water. Her tracks went out to the left. They were very prominent in the desert sand. I was standing at the back of the tracking troop with my professional hunter and a tracker. For whatever reason I looked to my right from where we came from and less than five yards away the lioness was crouched behind a little scrub brush, almost totally hidden. She could have easily killed one or more of us in a split-second but she decided to turn tail and run. We tracked her for over ten miles, and she backtracked us at least three times we were aware of. She was following us following her. That was some unnerving stuff, y'all. So, what's my point? Well, it is this: I don't want you to be paranoid but you're being followed by Satan. Yes, you have the victory in Christ. Yes, you have the Armor of God. However, if you're silly, unguarded, and not sober-minded, you will probably get eaten and turned into lion scat.

Five. Serving God now, when you're a young man, will save you from unnecessary and massive heartaches, regrets, and demonic bondages. I got converted when I was twenty-one after nearly a decade of drug and alcohol abuse and criminal activity. The crowd I was running with blew off my appeals to them to repent, turn to Christ, and turn their back on sin and Satan. The carnage several of them lived through up into their fifties was brutal. Some of my old buddies did get converted but the hell they underwent was the stuff of Stephen King novels.

So, remember at the beginning of this lecture when I said that my wife and I went to a party with wealthy and pretty people and a young, non-Christian, businessman advised me to not take life so seriously when I told him I wanted to preach The Gospel? Two years ago, he died an abysmal drunk. That was the fruit of him not taking his life so seriously. My advice to you, young men, is to follow Paul's admonition and be sober-minded and joyfully and wholeheartedly take your life seriously.

1. Paul writes in Titus 2 that young men are to be self-restrained and take life seriously. Is that something that is common today? Why do you think that's the case?

2. Have you known anyone to die young? Did they have any advance warning, or were they blindsided?

3. *Memento mori* is an old-school Latin phrase people use to remind themselves that death always lurks just around the corner. Would you be mak-

ing different choices if you really believed there was a chance you could drop dead tomorrow? Give some examples of what would be different.

4. What are some of the most common/dangerous traps where Satan can leverage being 'unserious' into a snare for young men?

Chapter 5. God's Grand Blueprint For Young Men.

Then God said, "Let Us make mankind in Our image, according to Our likeness; and let them rule over the fish of the sea and over the birds of the sky and over the livestock and over all the earth, and over every crawling thing that crawls on the earth." So God created man in His own image, in the image of God He created him; male and female He created them. God blessed them; and God said to them, "Be fruitful and multiply, and fill the earth, and subdue it; and rule over the fish of the sea and over the birds of the sky and over every living thing that moves on the earth."

– Genesis 1:26-28

There it is young warriors. Genesis 1:26-28. This is what the Father, Son, and the Holy Ghost intended men to be.

Are y'all ready to take a jaunt through these three verses with me? You are? Well, good. Let's get giddy up then.

Here's seven ditties from those three verses that define a man's masculinity from God's perspicacious perch.

Yo, dads: The following is what you should be preaching and modeling for your boys.

Ditto regarding pastors modeling this to the young men in the church.

Men were created to be …

1. Wild.

2. Leaders.

3. Cultivators.

4. Multipliers.

5. Dragonslayers.

6. Wise.

7. Reflectors of the Majesty of God.

ONE: MEN WERE CREATED TO BE WILD.

Adam lived around wildlife. Lots of fish and animals.

What does that say to the indoor boy Christian male? Does that have any relevance to a sassy twenty-first-century Christian hipster? I think it speaks volumes.

Back in Miami a smarmy religious lady once asked me: "Why do you hunt and fish so much?"

I answered her, "Well, Broomhilda, one reason I do is because it takes me away from snotty-nosed people like you and your dumb irrelevant questions that are simply none of yo' bizness."

Look, man: Adam wasn't an indoor soy boy growing man boobs, staring at propaganda and porn videos sent to him from China while he tanked up on snacks loaded down with trans fatty acids.

Adam was more like Bear Grylls.

Adam was at home with the feral.

God wanted his creative order to carve a mark on His primal man.

God wanted His first boy brought up in undomesticated surroundings. The feral fashioned something in Adam, that video games, Starbucks lattes, and smartphones just couldn't provide to the charge under His tutelage.

Yes, God's earthly second-in-command was directly connected to the Spirit of the Wild. Adam lived in primitive partnership with untamed beasts, birds, big lizards, and monster sharks. This is the way it was. And God said, "It is good!" Imagine that: good being equated to having no anti-bacterial gel, no bike helmets, no social media, no poodles, no motorized scooters, no concrete, and no boy bands. I know this doesn't sound like "paradise" for postmodern pantywaists that are immoral, lazy, stupid and fat, but it was God's -- and His primitive son's -- idea of "Yippee Land."

So, what do we learn from this preliminary little Bible nugget, children? The lesson is clear: if you want to step away from the pusillanimous pack, then you might want to get beyond the pavement, and let the created order carve its mark into your soul.

I don't have boys, but we made certain when our two alpha teenaged females were growing up that they had a regular dose of the irregular wild. Our lives consisted of large quantities of surfing in shark infested waters, biking in the backwoods, workouts on the beach, hunting in the sweltering swamps of the everglades for wild boar, fishing the brimming waters of South Florida, and treks into the African bush. Why did my wife and I make the financial commitment and time-laden efforts to get away from the tidy and the comfortable? Well, call us weak; but we need it for our souls, our sanity, and our spirits in this increasingly crappy culture we dwell in. The spiritual and ethical moorings that nature affords us cannot be found in the tame and lame wastelands of civilization.

So, take the time, young men, to venture away from the city, away from the prissy and predictable, and watch what happens to your spirit when you separate from the sassy and you're forced to interface with the primal. It is magical.

TWO: MEN WERE CREATED TO BE LEADERS.

God's initial earth boy was born to dominate creation and to exercise authority over the planet. God designed His first terrestrial son to be a leader, to take charge, to exert influence. God didn't construct Adam to be a passive clod, some indolent, handout addict who abnegates his responsibility to other people or institutes; but rather, Adam was to be a bold and imaginative chief. This is the very thing the man-haters hate in men and are trying desperately to curb in your kid, namely, this can-do spirit.

Lionhearted

Young squire, under God's governance, you should seek to lead, compete, and conquer. The first thing to conquer and the most important thing to dominate is your self-obsessed, lower cortex, monkey brain of fleshly delights. From there you can dominate your filthy bedroom, mow the yard, compete in sports, and master some form of arts or science. In addition to subduing those inward and outward challenges, you should learn to lead righteously and courageously.

Look, according to the scripture, you're a natural born leader who will naturally want to control. It is only, and I mean only, when you're cowed by abusive authority, Ritalin-ed out of your brains and *cojones*, or indoctrinated to believe this God-given behavior is bad, that turns you into a follower, a veritable sheeple of stupid cultural mores, folding to high pressure peers and ideological bunkum. With the leader funk removed from your trunk, you become tofu for the man-haters. Now you become malleable little spongy play-things and are no longer steel-willed competitive leaders. Yes, you become nice, placid cooperators and doormats to fools and foes. God never intended a young man to be this type of doe-eyed squishy mess.

Therefore, young man, your duties are two-fold: 1) Unleash the leadership beast within your life, and 2) Have more mature and accomplished leaders in your life superintend you to make sure you don't get weird. Who'll ensure your leadership skills are used for the purpose of justice, truth, provision, and protection? Take God's lead on how to exercise dominion and how to be a constructive and masculine Christian leader.

THREE: MEN WERE CREATED TO BE CULTIVA-
TORS.

The Garden of Eden that God allotted Adam was not
some hotel room that he was licensed to trash, but a place
he was "to tend and keep" (Gen. 2.16). Adam was to cultivate that which he had subdued. With his leadership came
the responsibility and accountability to God to take that
which was under his care and make it better. Can you say
better? I knew you could.

This means, young man, you're expected in your role
in your family and in this game of life to enhance that
which is good and to not whiz on everything people have
worked hard for. Whatever gets tossed to you is to be
brought into greater order, usefulness, and beauty. This is
your job as a young man. You're to do it. Not the government, not mommy, not your nanny, not your church. You,
as a young man, are here to cultivate that which is holy,
just, and good. You're here to make this planet shine. And
you should feel really weird if you don't make things better and God's kingdom to prosper.

Yes, young man who liveth in the God-blessed testosterone fog, you are not free to use, abuse, abandon, desert,
ignore, overlook, disregard, forget, avoid, or neglect that
which gets placed under your care. You are to cultivate
greatness, order, beauty, and God's glory everywhere you
go. It's called taking responsibility to make certain things
don't suck.

FOUR: MEN WERE CREATED TO SLAY DRAG-
ONS.

In Genesis chapter three, when our first parents got
tossed out of the sweet haven of Eden's crib, God said

He was going to redeem this sinful mess by raising up a Son who is to crush the serpent. Where God's first man, Adam, blew it by not being the dragonslayer, His Second Man, the Last Adam, took care of business and turned the malevolent slithering one into a grease stain.

This means, young warrior, you're to grow up to be a mini-me slayer of serpents. You're not to be a pacifist in the face of evil. You're not to roll over and wet yourself when confronted by evil. You're not to play the wimp when faced with wicked situations.

Look, I know it's hard for some of us to square Christ with slaying dragons – given all the androgynous, soft-focused paintings of Jesus that we've had jammed into our psyches for the last few centuries. However, if you take the scripture straight, Jesus was an eschatological warrior who has great joy in giving the devil hell. No matter how hard the softies try to make Christ out to be the benign, bearded lady raconteur, the exegetical fact remains: if you take the holy text in its entirety, He does not fit into the effete mold.

Therefore, my young brothers, get used to confronting nonsense – first and foremost in yourself. Gear up to be a fighter and defender of that which is just and good according to the Word of God and not CNN. You're growing up in difficult times that demand that you're able to deal with "snakes." As a Christian young man your duty and calling is not only to be nice, but also to be strong, sacrificial, bold, and courageous

FIVE: MEN WERE CREATED TO BE WISE.

Dear Young Dudes: Here's a message you'll never

hear at Youth Group, namely, make certain that you're the most well-read young man on your block.

If you stay dumb (and I'm not referring to people with learning disabilities) then you boost the malicious stereotype that the anti-theists are shoving down society's throat, and you unwittingly set the stage for a worse *mañana*, at least as far as masculinity goes.

Therefore, young warriors understand that …

1. Serious studying is not just for Poindexters and geeks.

2. Studying, learning, and holding intellectual discussions are all part of being masculine.

3. The intellectual target you're aiming to strike shouldn't look like some famous moron on social media; but rather more like King David, William Wallace, and/or Sir Winston Churchill.

4. It takes tomatoes to tackle the various sciences and no matter what your goofy friends think, serious study is not for wussies. As a matter of fact, it is just the opposite. Reading, meditating, gaining understanding and knowledge, and staying abreast of what has happened and what is happening on this world's stage is so hard that the effeminate, the little Sally's; the prancing, petite and effete evangelicals won't do it; they actually avoid it like an impenitent big girl does Jenny Craig.

5. God intends for you to be sharp and to not be

a bastardization of His great gender. Therefore, go to work on getting a killer library. Spend the cash! The rowdy realm of ideas and debate can be just as fun as any sport.

6. In fact, one of my greatest joys is when I get to go toe-to-toe on the radio, TV, or over dinner with a Marxist or an anti-theist. Yeah, it is right up there with hunting Africa's green hills, nearly.

Finally, imagine the angst when Hollywood and the multitudinous, universities can no longer play the stooge card when it comes to you because you have engaged your brain and have not opted for anti-intellectualism. Indeed, being a sharp, solid, and smart young man for God's glory will delight the Father's heart and sour our enemy's stomach because you don't fit their anti-intellectual description of Christian men.

SIX: MEN WERE CREATED TO REFLECT THE MAJESTY OF GOD.

Genesis One states young men are to be image-bearers of the Godhead. Yep, you're to be a reflector of the majesty of God. Yikes, eh? Most young Christian dudes sucking oxygen on this planet are image-bearers and reflectors of whatever twit is currently the flavor of the month in our sullied society. Most are conformed to the world and not transformed from it. God's design for you is that you showcase His nature and character and not what is hip and groovy, you dig?

One great way to not turn into a male popinjay is to take serious stock of the masculine role models you're around. You're going to imitate someone, so make certain it isn't some deceived dandy. This is not rocket science. But it is a science. It's simple: if you don't want to be emasculated or macho-stupid, be careful who you emulate as you schlep this third rock from the sun. Monkey see, monkey do.

Here are several role models to add as standard bearers to your life.

Jesus Christ. I know some of you are thinking, "Uh, duh." Allow me to explain what I mean. When I say "Jesus should be your main role model" I mean the Jesus of the scriptures and not the neutered beard-lady "Jesus" that is popular amongst gooey evangelicals. Read deeply about what He said and did and then ask the Holy Ghost to empower you to follow His lead. A great place to get a grip on Christ's masculine gruffness is my book, If Masculinity's Toxic, Call Jesus Radioactive. After reading that weighty tome you'll never see Jesus the same way.

In addition to Christ's glorious example, here are some warriors to mimic…

For praise and worship, do it like King David. He wasn't some inhibited evangelical. David was a noisy, shouting, clapping, and dancing tornadic ball of energy during corporate worship and when he was alone with God. And for guys who think behaving like that isn't masculine, please remember that David was a mighty warrior and I guarantee he could kick your backside. David embodied a bold, wild, and free form of worship that God preserved in Holy Writ as a blueprint for believers. Copy David's glide path and see what happens.

For faith, follow Abraham's lead. When Abe was well past his prime. When his wedding tackle was completely defunct with regard to reproduction, God told him he was going to father multitudes and Abraham believed God in that hope against hope situation.

For rebellion against bad government, follow Moses' lead. Moses didn't take Pharaoh's enslaving crap. Moses' motif was rebellion to tyrants is obedience to God. Yep, Moses was not some compliant stooge of The Political Machine that enslaved God's people to bad ideas.

For rebellion against bad religion, follow John The Baptist's lead. If you were a self-righteous jackanape, who thought you were better than others because of your religious traditions, John would publicly lambaste you with prophetic glee. My book, John The Baptist: A Rude Awakening Precedes A Great Awakening showcases in one-hundred and fifty-four pages why God honored and used that wild critter. You'd be wise to lather, rinse, and repeat how Johnny lived before the Audience of One.

The aforementioned examples, as you know, have all passed away. That said, through the scripture, they still bear an "image" that is well worth reflecting. Hello. In addition to them, seek out living masculine role models who showcase the classic masculine traits of being a provider, protector, hunter, and hero under God's governance.

Garner to yourself, young men, male role models who're masters in their field. Who follow hard after everything that God says is holy, just, and good. Or you could hang out with your rudderless peers, your drunken uncle, and your radical Marxist aunt and see how that goes for you.

---

1. Why is it especially important in our current culture to take the time to get out into nature and "touch grass" in Gen-Z speak?

2. What aspect of nature most inspires the divine sense of "awe" in you — mountains, deserts, oceans, the night sky, a wide horizon the strength of an animal, the beauty of a natural vista, or a spectacular sunset?

3. What part of God's world or human society do you have a strong desire to "make better"?

4. Where does culture tell you to look for mentors and role models? What makes Doug's vision different? Can you think of some examples in your church or community that would be the kind of role models Doug is talking about?

5. For any older guys reading this — are you living the life of that kind of role model? If yes, are you passing the torch to the next generation? If no, what changes do you need to make to become one — and how soon are you willing to make them?

Lionhearted

Chapter 6. Slackers Will Hate This Chapter.

"As for every matter of wisdom and understanding about which the king consulted them, he found them [that's Daniel and his three young male amigos] ten times better than all the magicians and conjurers who were in all his realm."

– Daniel 1:20

Wow. Imagine that. Christian young men (teenagers) who're ten times better than the unscrubbed general populace. Yep, that's what the Holy Spirit preserved in the book of Daniel for all of us poor dullards to read, weep, and aspire toward.

Now that's a tall order, young warriors.

Ten times better than your heathen competition?

No doubt some are thinking, "Garsh ... that's not nice, Jesus. Why would you make the standard to influence an anti-theistic environment like Babylon so hard? I thought Christianity was all about getting stuff, having you bless all our selfish wishes, and then going to heaven to eat ice cream with Moses as we play harps, wear white peignoirs, and lounge on clouds?"

By the way, that accolade of being "ten times better" was given by a very wicked king and not Danny's mommy nor his doting youth pastor.

Oh, and here's another aside, in case you've never been around powerful and wicked people: they don't give a rat's backside about what you believe. They care about how you perform, how you can benefit them, and not if you see angels, wear Christian T-shirts, and can speak in tongues. Daniel and his buddies' skill set simply blew Neb away. They were ten times better than all the rest of the men in Nebuchadnezzar's court. Just let that sink in a bit ...

Here's a question for you, the young Christian male: I wonder if your "evil" boss or your "godless" workmates or your "unsaved" family or your "lost" neighbors, or pretty much every "unwashed heathen" who interfaces with you on a regular basis can say of your person, your work, your craft, your family, your marriage, your appearance, your demeanor and in regard to your wisdom that you are "ten times better" than all the "estranged from the covenant" peeps who're your contemporaries?

Ouch, eh?

Nebuchadnezzar said that about Danny and the boys, and that, young man, is what you should be aspiring towards, namely: outperforming the lost competition in the practical and honorable stuff of life and work.

Christianity hasn't put too much stock in proclaiming excellence in all our endeavors. No, indeed, we put forth haggard garbage and sloppy lives and then we stand back and are aghast that no one wants to listen to us talk about Jesus.

Why should they listen to such a person? Jesus, evidently, hasn't made that big of a difference in their life so ... why should they follow their lead? It's kind of like what Jonathan Edwards' sang about back in 1971, "But he can't even run his own life, I'll be damned if he'll run mine ..."

Pedro put it this way ...

> *"Therefore, putting aside all malice and all deceit and hypocrisy and envy and all slander, like newborn babies, long for the pure milk of the word, so that by it you may grow in respect to salvation ... But you are a chosen race, a royal priesthood, a holy nation, a people for God's own possession, so that you may proclaim the excellencies of Him who has called you out of darkness into His marvelous light ..."*
>
> – 1Peter 2:1-2,9 (NASB)

Peter, via the inspiration of the Holy Spirit, said the whole point of our getting converted was not going to heaven but an earthly, yea, bodily, proclamation of the excellencies of God.

Jesus spun it in this manner:

"Let your light shine before men in such a way that they may see your good works, and glorify your Father who is in heaven."

– Matthew 5:16 (NASB)

Good works (operative word "good"), equates God the Father getting glorified. Shoddy works? Eh ... not so much.

So, what is excellence? Well, excellence simply defined is:

The quality of being outstanding or extremely good. Synonyms include: distinction, quality, superiority, brilliance, greatness, merit, caliber, eminence, preeminence, supremacy; skill, talent, virtuosity, accomplishment, mastery.

Does that define your person and work?

For those who're thinking that excellence is some form of elitism that only the hoity-toity care about and it's not an essential and expected quality for all Christian young men, allow me to slay that notion by stating that excellence isn't about arrogance and ego, but about love for God and an act of worship.

Here's what I mean ...

"Whatever you do, do your work heartily, as for the Lord rather than for men, knowing that from the Lord you will receive the reward of the inheritance. It is the Lord Christ whom you serve."

– Colossians 3: 23-24 (NASB)

Lionhearted

Pablo said our work, whatever it may be, is to be done "heartily" (literally: with our soul) unto God and not just for men. That smacks of excellence to *moi*. Does it to you? *Oui*? Good.

Consequently, hearty and excellent, well-done and well-made work, is not something that's vanity or an aside to the "more spiritual" matters of evangelism, saying prayers and singing churchy songs.

Hard and smart work is worship; it is to God and for God. Can you imagine actually presenting what you work on, whether it's goods, services, or merchandise unto Jesus Christ? Do you think He'd be impressed? Do you think He'd be insulted? Do you think He'd say, *"Oy vey"* and slowly leave your demonstration to go get a glass of wine to try to cheer Himself up after watching your presentation?

I'm afraid many young Christian males would be too embarrassed to show their work to Jesus because it's half-hearted garbage. If your work is junk, I guarantee your supposed "personal relationship" with Jesus is also junk. One cannot divorce the two.

For Daniel and his pals, being "just okay" or "good enough" or "nice" was not good enough for them. God deserved their best and the wicked King honored only excellence and, boy howdy ... did those young boys supply excellence in spades.

The bottom line, with a lot of folks outside Jesus' fold is, "Excellence talks and bullocks walks."

Nebuchadnezzar paid attention to Daniel's counsel because he simply crushed the competition.

I think the world would give a big ear to what we have to say if our wisdom, work, and ways just simply amazed people.

> *"Do you see a man skilled in his work? He will stand before kings; He will not stand before obscure men."*

> – Proverbs 22:29 (NASB)

---

1. Does Doug's call to a life of excellence give you an exemption if your boss happens to be a jerk? Explain your answer.

2. If you asked the non-Christian people you know, would they think Christians are examples of excellence or half-baked slackers?

3. If you were in a situation where your life (or livelihood) depended on the competence of a hired expert, would you hit up Google reviews or a look within a network of Christian businesses? Why?

4. What would happen to our cruddy culture if Christians were to step up into the rarified air of a God-honoring, Daniel-like excellence?

Lionhearted

Chapter 7. How To Operate When Life Throat Punches You.

The years 2020 - 2021+ were devastating to millions of people.

Lots of stress, to say the least.

Lives and businesses were crushed.

Nefarious forces were afoot making peoples' lives a living hell.

Oddly enough, for me personally, those two-plus years weren't nearly as bad as the slop I went through from 2016 through 2018. Those years stretched me like a bungee cord with a big woman on the other end of it.

In 2016, Facebook began to shadowban posts from our wildly popular news portal, ClashDaily.com (300M+

page views). This cut our ad revenue in half. In 2017 the foes at Facebook aggressively started to block our Facebook page (2M followers with a page reach of 10-20M per week) which further crushed our bottom line. Which was a very nice bottom line, mind you. In October of 2018, Facebook banned me for life. Other ad sources jumped onto the woke wagon and greatly demonetized our website because we stumped for a Judeo-Christian worldview, common sense, The Constitution, The Bill of Rights, and The Declaration of Independence and we did it with an irreverent sense of humor.

Everything me, my wife, my business partners, and writers had worked our butts off for, and succeeded greatly at, was ... poof ... gone ... all because of our aversion to kowtowing to the big tech liberal thought police.

I thought I was going to ride this great news portal we'd created off into the sunset. I was wrong. We were crushed. To say those days were hectic is to greatly understate the pain and the unknowing of "what's next, Lord?"

Our lives were under stress. That sweet income was kaput.

However, through that epic stress, our faith grew greatly (James 1:2-6).

God came through in a powerful way, just as He promised (Ps. 37:25).

Like He promised, God did exceedingly and abundantly beyond all we could ask or imagine (Eph. 3:20,21).

The following message, based on Psalm 4:1, became very true to my life during that grueling spate of yucky years. I held on to that verse and many others when we were getting the shiitake mushrooms kicked out of us. If you're going through a rough patch right now, I hope it ministers to you the way it did for me. If you're not going through a hard time now, file this message away because you will. Pain is a guarantee in this life.

King David said, "Hear me when I call, O God of my righteousness: thou hast enlarged me when I was in distress; have mercy upon me, and hear my prayer." – Psalm 4:1 (KJV).

Check out how other translators render that verse ...

... When I call, answer me, O God of my righteousness: in pressure thou hast enlarged me; (DAR)

... "Whenever I was in distress, you enlarged me." (TPT)

... Answer my prayers, O True God, the righteous, who makes me right. I was hopelessly surrounded, and You rescued me. Once again hear me; hide me in Your favor; bring victory in defeat and hope in hopelessness. (VOICE)

Focus on these goodies God gave David when David was going through life's woodchipper.

"Thou hast enlarged me when I was in distress."

"In pressure thou hast enlarged me."

"I was hopelessly surrounded, and You rescued me. Once again hear me; hide me in Your favor; bring victory in defeat and hope in hopelessness."

David said he grew through his pain and that God enlarged him and rescued him, bringing victory in defeat and hope in hopelessness, hiding David in His favor.

Growth through pain.

Imagine that.

Here's an FYI to the young Christian males who aspire to grow in their faith: David's growth in God was preceded by this thing called "distress."

For those of you not hip to the word distress, it means extreme pain, a state of danger, or desperate need. In other words, the crap hit the fan in David's life (many, many times) and yet, David grew.

It's a funny thing about crap. We've got a spot in our massive backyard that, for whatever reason, our dogs like to fertilize. That little patch of Bermuda that they regularly pop a squat on is taller and greener than the rest of the grass that surrounds it. Why is it more radiant and healthy? Well, aside from the sunshine and rain, the only difference between it and the other turf is it gets pooped and peed on a lot, as did David (metaphorically speaking, of course).

The reason David knew God so well was because he was constantly under attack either by God's people or God's enemies. You see, David actually needed God. David's life was one storm/battle after the other. If he wasn't dealing with external enemies he was dealing with his internal demons. David had a target on his back and the devil constantly tried to take him out. Thus, David, unlike most Christians, clung to God for deliverance and not

MasterCard, Visa, American Express, mommy or daddy, or prescription drugs.

Through all the stuff David plowed through, he didn't just barely make it. He grew like a weed. He thrived. He experienced God on a level that most Christians never will because most of the church does everything in its power to avoid pain and stress. David embraced the pain, relied heavily on God, and came to know God's person and works in an amazing way that we're fortunate to behold, especially in the Psalms.

David says in Psalm 4:1 and in Psalm 119:67, 68, and 71 that the distress and affliction that he went through, some via the hand of others and some created by his own stupid mistakes enlarged him and schooled him into keeping God's word. Hello.

Check it out ...

"Before I was afflicted I went astray, But now I keep Your word. You are good and You do good; Teach me Your statutes... It is good for me that I was afflicted, So that I may learn Your statutes."

– Psalm 119: 67,68, 71 (NASB)

Please note -- after the pain, at least in David's life, came holy growth and a more circumspect walk with God.

David said that the distress and affliction allowing God is "good" and "does good." Yes, little Dinky. David said God is and does good even when He allows for distress and affliction in our lives.

David, after getting jackhammered in life, didn't curse God.

He didn't join some radical anti-theistic Marxist cabal.

He didn't become some pouty college dropout who gets a neck tattoo that says, "God sucks."

He didn't get on Instagram and start caterwauling, "Why me, Lord?"

He had the maturity to roll with the punches and to understand that for God to grow us weird critters up and into something He's not ashamed of (Heb. 2:11) sometimes, oftentimes, He's gotta pinch our gelatinous and insidious flesh (Heb. 12:4-11).

David's distress and affliction didn't lead him to blame or get bitter at God. It led him to personal growth and a closer relationship with his Creator and that's exactly how we should respond when life, for whatever reason, dropkicks us into left field.

A few years ago, I contemplated taking Brazilian Jiu-Jitsu lessons at the ripe old age of 55. Both my daughters are Gracie/Valente black belts in BJJ. So, I asked them what would be the first thing I'd learn if I started training. Would I learn some intricate UFC submission moves? What about headbutting? Or how to eye-gouge? Or where to bite my opponent? Or hair-pulling? Or groin attacks and small joint manipulations?!? My girls were like, "Uh ... no dad. The first thing you'll learn is how to fall." How to fall? Who the heck wants to learn how to fall? That sounded about as fun as kissing my sister.

For the BJJ practitioner, their advantages are readily showcased when the fight goes to the ground. In other words, falling down ain't a bad thing at all. For the BJJ scrapper it's exactly where they want to go.

Lionhearted

When David had life knock him to the ground, he too saw that as an advantageous place to be because he understood that lowly position is a place enlargement of his person and his work and a great place to know God more deeply and see Him work more dramatically.

Herewith, are seven little nuggets on how to steady oneself for growth in God and in life when (not if) you get kicked in the teeth by some terrible trial.

1. Stay objective. David said in Ps. 42:5 (NASB), "Why are you in despair, my soul? And why are you restless within me? Wait for God, for I will again praise Him For the help of His presence, my God." I don't know if you caught this or not, but David is talking to David. David is taking an objective stance against his subjective self. Effectively, David is telling himself to quit being a whiny wuss. David's talking himself up and out of his little slough of despond he's mired in. Y'know ... It's great to have friends and family for encouragement but we've gotta learn to do this trick all by our lonesome or we could self-sabotage. Stay focused after getting pummeled. If you're still breathing, there's still hope....

2. Don't freak out. Who wants to be remembered as the freakazoid who's known for panicking? Not me, *señorita*. When you act out of fear, that's when you make some mondo mistakes (Deut. 20:8). Remember when fear tries to take you

over, that God would never give you a spirit of fear but of power, love, and a sound mind (2Tim. 1:7). Satan breeds fear, not Jehovah.

3. Be careful how you "see." Can you see the good in the bad? If you can, you're a rare monkey in these days of mass delusional psychotics. When Saul and Israel saw Goliath, they saw a giant that was too big to kill. When teenage David saw Goliath, he saw a giant that was too big to miss (1Sam. 17:45-47). How do you "see" your obstacles? Too big? Too scary? Or do you view your setbacks as mere speed bumps in light of your awesome God who's even more big and scary than anything life and Satan can toss at you?

4. Get gritty. (Deut. 23:1-6) Speaking of speed bumps, American Christians flip out when they go over mole hills in the Garden of Eden. Gritty, we're not. We're missing a tad bit of the plucky spirit that the early church had. Getting knocked down is par for the Christian course. Get up. Dust yourself off. Now, move forward in faith.

5. Be better than the godless. (Matt. 6:25-33) Jesus said in Matt. 6:25-33 that the Christian should be distinct from the godless in that they do not share the unwashed masses' mass delusional psychosis over food, clothing, and shelter because the believer understands that if God feeds little birds and dresses up flowers with useless beauty then

He'll take care of His followers. Hello.

6. Say "whatever" when Satan spews fear, terror, dread, panic, and "fake news" into your noggin about your future (1Pet. 5:8). Satan's a liar who spawns fear and accuses Christians. Which means, duh, the Christian shouldn't believe him. Declare God's promises over your life and not Satan's doom and gloom garbage. Defy el Diablo. Defy your enemies. Prove everyone wrong.

7. Fix what you can fix. Say stuff in your life is way out of control with regard to what you can throttle. You can't fix it. Mama can't fix it. Your buddies can't fix it, etc. If that's true, you can always go to work on yourself. You always have an open door to God. There's nothing keeping you from giving of your time, talent, and treasure. There's nothing keeping you from loving more, caring more and being available for whatever the hand of God needs doing. Unless you're dead, of course. Indeed, there's a ton of stuff you can do in the midst of the junk you currently can't do anything about.

Lastly, the suckiest suckful suck years of 2016-2018 when we lost our business due to Herr Zuckerberg's fascistic edicts, were actually a Godsend. Now, looking back, I thank Him for allowing this pain to happen in my life because now, though not perfect, I'm in a way better spot in life now than I was back then.

Consider it a sheer gift, friends, when tests and challenges come at you from all sides. You know that under pressure, your faith-life is forced into the open and shows its true colors. So don't try to get out of anything prematurely. Let it do its work so you become mature and well-developed, not deficient in any way.

If you don't know what you're doing, pray to the Father. He loves to help. You'll get his help, and won't be condescended to when you ask for it. Ask boldly, believingly, without a second thought. People who "worry their prayers" are like wind-whipped waves. Don't think you're going to get anything from the Master that way, adrift at sea, keeping all your options open. -- James 1:2-8 (MSG)

---

1. When the bottom falls out of your life -- really falls out -- what are some good and bad decisions people turn to in coping with it? What are some of your defaults? Which of these can be swapped out for better options?

2. Are you resilient by personality, or do you have to work at it?

3. What steps have you been taking to make yourself more ready to handle a crisis? If your answer is "none", what are your next steps to do so in the future?

Lionhearted

4. Doug's crisis stressor, where he found out what he's really made of, was business/money. What worst-case scenario would put you through the wringer? Where would you turn if everything hit the fan in your life?

Chapter 8. Monkey See. Monkey Do.

Dear Young Christian Dude: How many truly biblically masculine friends do you have? I'm talking about heat-seeking, truth-seeking missiles that are accomplished in life... spiritually... physically... mentally... and materially?

In addition, are the older men you interface with men of renown in regard to that which is holy, just, and good? If your answer to the aforementioned was … uh … a scant few to none, then you, my little amigo, have got a problem. It's a fixable problem, but it's a problem, nonetheless.

Here's another question, fair sunshine, how many of your buddies are chestless goofballs? I'm talkin' about veritable sponges of culture, biblically dumb as a bag of hammers, addicted to social media and they take notes while watching CNN, Disney+, and Netflix?

Lastly, in regard to your Youth Pastor, is he nicer than Christ? Does his hair put the gel in evangelical? Is he over-ebullient? Does he come off more like a game show host than a scary prophet? As Mario Murillo would ask, is he more into skinny jeans, big screens, and smoke machines than he's into teaching you the hard truths of scripture that'll equip you to boldly stand in this evil day? If your answer to the two aforesaid inquiries was in the affirmative, then guess what you are, Slingblade? If you guessed, "doomed to be a politically correct insipid Christian dolt" -- you guessed right.

You are, and will become, like the ones you run with. If you disbelieve that advice then go ahead, follow your lackluster buddies for the next two decades and see how that works out for you.

The Bible is replete with warnings to the believer about the danger of hanging out with fools, both non-Christian and Christian alike. Yep, confessed, so-called, "Christians" can be harmful to your life if their practices and beliefs are not backed up by this thing called, The Word of God.

Check out these warnings in Proverbs ...

He who walks with wise men will be wise,
But the companion of fools will suffer harm.

– Proverbs 13:20 (NASB)

Leave the presence of a fool,
Or you will not discern words of knowledge.

– Proverbs 14:7 (NASB)

Lionhearted

Do not associate with a man given to anger;
Or go with a hot-tempered man,
Or you will learn his ways
And find a snare for yourself.

$\qquad$ – Proverbs 22:24-25 (NASB)

Do not enter the path of the wicked
And do not proceed in the way of evil men.
Avoid it, do not pass by it;
Turn away from it and pass on.

$\qquad$ – Proverbs 4:14-15 (NASB)

A man of violence entices his neighbor
And leads him in a way that is not good.

$\qquad$ – Proverbs 16:29 (NASB)

He who keeps the law is a discerning son,
But he who is a companion of gluttons humiliates
his father.

$\qquad$ – Proverbs 28:7 (NASB)

The Holy Spirit makes it abundantly clear, in those few verses, that if you hang with idiots, you'll become an idiot.

If you need further proof that I'm not a bubble off-level then google, "Bad Company and the Bible" and see what pops up.

Yes, Junior, if your life reeks and you're getting the stuffing kicked out of you by the world, the flesh, and the devil, it could be because you're palling around with the pusillanimous. Like begets like. Fire begets fire. And stupid begets stupid. Get it? Got it? Good.

Oh, by the way, you cannot blame your buddies for your ignominious glide path. You chose your influencers. So that's on you. This realization that it's your fault is good because as you chose badly you can now choose wisely. That's assuming, of course, that you truly want to get a life.

So, say you do wish to get out of your sad state of affairs, and you now wish to run with men who live in the rarified, successful air, of the testosterone-laden fog that God hardwired men to dwell in. That, obviously, is a great and smart move but I have to warn you ... it won't be easy. Here's why: Accomplished people will not want to hang around you unless you've thoroughly repented from being *magna cum* mamma's boy and have proven you've been consistent on this radical new path for at least... oh... the last five years.

However difficult it will be for you to both leave the flock of the rudderless you schlepp with and make new relationships with solid people who'll probably stiff-arm you unless you pay them money, the first "must" you must do to decidedly move the heck away from Wussville and get on the grand path to Mantown is to get around serious and successful men of God. Their indomitable spirit will jump off on you.

Here are two more little ditties that'll help you morph into an epic giantslayer instead of a pathetic guilt manipulator …

Number One. Read biographies and watch documentaries of people who went through way worse hell than you ever have or will and pray to God you get a scintilla of their warrior spirit.

Number Two. In addition, fill your house, or room, with art that inspires you not to be a male Karen. For instance, in my house, I surround myself with my artwork, which primarily consists of Africa's Big Five; the grandest and most dangerous critters known to walk God's green globe. I also have portraits of great leaders like King David, William Wallace, and Sir Winston Churchill. They feed my spirit. When I start to feel like a timid titmouse, I look at these great men, women, and animals, then say to myself, "Self, you're being rather toady today." I then punch myself in the face and then get busy kicking butt versus sitting on my backside. Remember, life imitates art. Therefore, don't get lame art. To pursue all of my available artwork go to DougGiles.Art.

You're welcome.

1. How do your most meaningful influences stack up to Doug's standards? Are they the kind of people you want to become? What about the people whose lives and examples you read about?

2. Can you think of examples of people you know who changed when they joined a new friend group? Discuss the positive/negative changes of that impact.

3. What is the last biography of a worthy role model you read? Did you read it to entertain yourself or to challenge yourself? What did you learn?

4. Who are your heroes? What do you admire most about them?

Lionhearted

Chapter 9. This Grand Trait Epitomizes Biblical Masculinity.

When one thinks of a Christian young male nowadays the word "hero" does not come to mind, by and large, generally speaking, now does it?

I know I didn't think, "hero", with regard to the churchy males I interfaced with when I was an honorary member and senior leader of the local West Texas branch of The Teenage Wasteland Club.

Matter of fact, the lack of heroism in the Christian male collective I came in contact with was a great deterrent to me getting converted. I wanted Christ, you see, as a lost young squab, but I did not want to become a backward-looking hamster. Oh, no.

At that stage of the game, I did not know the Bible was replete with heroes and heroism because I never really read it. All I knew about Christianity and masculinity was from the dead-fish, weak handshakes I received from the nice boys who had fish stickers on their notebooks.

When I could no longer resist God's irresistible grace, I formally came into the fold at the ripe old age of twenty-one and found that all my fears about an effeminized flock were spot on.

What I found were weeping, hugging, and scared of the world retreatist males who were not looking to beard a false prophet, or slay a dragon but rather, they were just longing to cope with the challenge of going over molehills in the garden of Eden.

Heroic they were not. Again, generally speaking.

The few and far between heroic and manly examples at my local church were usually foreign missionaries, successful businessmen, righteous activists, street preachers, prison ministers, and college campus evangelists who'd regularly do outreaches, in the open air, with aggressive anti-theistic crowds. Now, those guys were cool. They took the scripture seriously and defended it passionately, in hostile environments, and had the best frickin' testimonies of God crushing devils and saving souls. They weren't afraid of playing the man amongst the sea of wilting Christian mommy-boys.

What I continue to find weird with the lack of heroism within young males is it is the main trait of the epic men and women of the scripture. Hello. They were not renowned for being nice and sweet gentle spokesmen for a fastidious religious do-gooder. They're God's protagonists because they usually, by His power, wiped out a massive foreign army, or nailed an evil captain's head to the ground, or smoked a foulmouthed uncircumcised gigantic mook with just a rock and a slingshot; or like Christ, they confronted Satan on a very empty stomach, and/or they took a whole bunch of lickings for their uncompromised faith and yet … they kept on ticking. Glory!

In the Old Testament, the hero was the mainstay of both the Children of Israel and their rivals. Without huge amounts of heroes, the various tribes would be toast; doomed, ransacked, and pillaged. The hero, young squire, was the central figure to the clan's survival, be they good or evil. Indeed, without heroes, whomever was out there trying to … you know … make it, would soon become this thing called, "dead meat" sans the necessary presence of the hardy hero.

Question. When's the last time you've heard a sermon on the church's desperate need for heroes?

Most current Christian messages are about being kind, being sweet, asking God for a new car, or a new job, or a new wife as God makes you rich and He makes everyone fawn over you via social media.

That's pretty much what's messaged, for the most part, in The First Church of The Sassy Saints. However, there be scant few sermons, nowadays, soliciting heroism within the formerly hallowed halls of the supposedly "called out ones." If you don't believe me, search "hero" in your church's sermon archives and see how many messages pop up on that topic.

Here's another thing they never told you at youth group: When God's people have decisively "gone wrong"

(Isa. 3:8) and have been "an affront to the Eternal (God), resisting His glorious presence." And "they flaunt their sins like Sodom" ... and "they don't even try to hide them (Isa. 3:9)" while "they persist in wrongdoing. (Isa. 3:11 VOICE)." One of the ways God brutally disciplines His people is by removing the hero from their midst and re-placing that masculine deterrent to evil with a bunch of chinless-wonder boys and lyin' ladies. Check it out ...

"See here! The Eternal, Commander of heavenly armies, will take away the supply of bread and water—the whole supply—from Jerusalem and Judah. He will take away their heroes and war-riors, judges and prophets ... and elders, He will take away their military officers and high-rank-ing officials.

– Isaiah 3:1-3 (VOICE)

Did you catch God's removal of the "heroes" and "warriors" part of that judgment? You did? Awesome. In case you were wondering, according to the scripture, that is not a good thing when that happens. That means that God has pulled His frontline of defense from His people making them oh-so-vulnerable to their mortal enemies. Yikes, eh?

With the removal of the hero and warrior, guess who God allows to lead in the hero's and warrior's absence? If you guessed a bunch of flaky young males and women with horrible, ungodly ideas -- you guessed right.

"And I will make mere lads their princes, And capricious children will rule over them, And the people will be oppressed, Each one by another, and each one by his neighbor; The youth will

storm against the elder And the inferior against the honorable ... O My people! Their oppressors are children, And women rule over them. O My people! Those who guide you lead you astray And confuse the direction of your paths.

– Isaiah 3:4-5; 12 (NASB)

Since God's people were acting the ungodly fool, blowing off His will and His way, God removes the heroes and replaces them with zeroes and when that happens, as you just read, all hell breaks loose upon His people. Yep, God's people get trampled by the enemy. They get completely stripped by demonic forces. That's what happens when the heroic spirit is gone. Evil rules the roost (Isa. 3:13-26)

One of the biggest reasons why I think heroism is more lost in our churches than Britney Spears is during a Jordan Peterson lecture is because God's not lauded as The Ultimate Butt Kicking Hero the scripture ubiquitously hails Him to be. Pastors emphasize Jesus being a "Personal Savior" and "Gentle Jesus, meek and mild" and de-emphasize He's a bold Dragon-Slayer and Hero, par excellence!

Listen to how Isaiah refers to God ...

As a hero throws himself into battle, the Eternal will take on His enemies; with passion, shouting out a deafening roar, He will power over them.

– Isaiah 42:13 (VOICE)

*The Eternal, your rescuing hero who formed
you before birth, declares, Eternal One: I am
the Eternal, Creator of all there is and will be. I
alone stretched out the heavens and spread out
the blue earth.*

— Isaiah 44:24 (VOICE)

*Israel: Our Savior, our hero -- the Eternal, Com-
mander of heavenly armies, by name—is the Holy
One of Israel!*

— Isaiah 47:4 (VOICE)

*I will turn your enemies' violence back on them-
selves, and they will suffer their own atrocities:
They will feed on their own flesh and drink their
own blood like wine. Then every person on earth
will know for certain that I, the Eternal, am your
Savior. I am your hero, the strong One of Jacob
from whom you come. I will rescue you, whatever
the price.*

— Isaiah 49:26 (VOICE)

*My hero who sets things right is near. Who would
dare to challenge me? Let's stand and debate this
head-to-head! Who would dare to accuse me? Let
him come near.*

— Isaiah 50:8 (VOICE)

Lionhearted

Finally, young male, if you have the Girlie-Man Malaise, one way to cure that illness is to meditate on God's character as a demonic butt-kicking Hero. Let that 411 roll around in your gray matter for the next several months and His indomitable Spirit will start to overcome your timid flesh. The resultant effect of that revelation will be this: when life calls you to do something heroic, you will "display strength and take action" (Dan. 11:32) instead of curling up in the fetal position and wetting your big, flighty Christian diaper. Can I get a witness?

----

1. What makes a "hero" different from ordinary Joes?

2. Before reading this, would you have considered "heroic" a trait Christian leaders should have?

3. Before reading this, did you ever stop to think of God Himself as being heroic?

Chapter 10. God's Will Makes You Like This Apex Predator.

Dear Young Men: To say that God is a generous giver is to understate a whopping big given.

Our two-cylinder gray matter will never be able to fully comprehend the magnitude of His generosity that He has lavished upon His former demon-driven, God-hating, thankless, fleshly, idol-worshiping enemies also known as you and me (Eph. 2:1-10).

God owes us nothing and yet decided to give us everything (Eph. 1:15-22).

According to the Bible, He's given His elect the following ...

His only begotten Son as our substitutionary sacrifice (John 3:16)

The gift of faith (Eph. 2:8)

The gift of repentance (Acts 5:31)

The gift of grace (Eph. 2:8)

The gift of the Word of God (Eph. 6:17)

"Seeing eyes" (Matt. 13:16)

"Hearing ears" (Matt. 13:16)

The Holy Spirit (Acts 2:38)

A glorious inheritance (Eph. 1:18)

Eternal life (Rom. 6:23)

A purpose on this planet (Rom. 8:28)

A part in His demon-thrashing organism called, The Church (Matt. 16:18)

Spiritual weapons and armor (Eph. 6:10-18)

Supernatural power (2Pet. 1:3)

Power over our flesh (Rom. 6:14)

The authority to bind demonic forces (Matt. 18:18)

His angelic army's assistance (Ps. 46:7)

24/7/365 access to His throne in prayer (Heb. 4:16)

Fruit of the Holy Spirit (Gal. 5:22)

Gifts of the Holy Spirit (1Cor. 12:4-11)

Lionhearted

Divine protection (Ps. 91)

Covenant promises (2Pet. 1:4)

Prosperity (3 John 2)

Health (3 John 2)

Healing (Isa. 53:5)

That's a pretty awesome little list that is far from an exhaustive account of what He's credited unto us simply because He's a good God and that's how He rolls (James 1:17).

There's one thing, however, if you have this character trait, then God did not give it to you.

Yep, if you're saddled with this crap, you didn't get it from Him.

You might have gotten this bent from talking too much to your aunt who's nuttier than a squirrel turd.

Or, perhaps, you now have this predilection because you listen to and believe what control freak politicians tell you.

Or, possibly, you are now saddled with this bunkum because you take notes while watching BSNBC.

Whatever the font from where you got this particular funk, it didn't come from our Heavenly Father.

So, what am I talking about, pray tell?

Well, you inquiring mind, I'm talking about the vomitus soup *du jour*, that a lot of Christians have eaten heapin' helpins of lately, namely: a spirit of fear.

Yes, Christians, who are called to fear not (Isa. 41:10) when in dire straits, tossed that notion aside around March 2020 and bought into what bureaucrats were selling us po' rubes, a thing Dr. Mark McDonald has deemed a "mass delusional psychosis", or what the Apostle Paul called, a spirit of fear (2Tim. 1:7).

Dear Church: What did Ray Davies teach us if he taught us anything at all, huh? He taught us that Paranoia Will Destroy Ya, and boy was he on point because fear of a bad cold and bad leaders did major, I said major, damage to the church, family, and state.

Hey, speaking of the church, show me one place in the scripture, Christian, where Jesus said to ...

1. Fear of getting a bad cold.

2. Obey a homunculus Italian "scientist" who tells you to skip Christmas this year and to wear a dirty rag over your face.

3. Shut your church down if a Mayor McCheese orders you to do it.

If you can show me one Bible verse that positively stumps for the aforementioned, I'll Riverdance in Borat's thong to an extended cut of The Doors smash hit, Riders On The Storm.

The Christian is never called to fear what this life tosses at them but to fear God and stand on His word instead (Lk. 12:4,5). Sadly, a lot of the church flunked that test when the Wuhan Wheezer was unleashed on us by China and fell prey to satanic anxiety.

Lionhearted

Fear is a sin, young man (Rev. 21:8). It's the antithesis of the Christian spirit of boldness (Prov. 28:1), hardiness (Heb. 10:32-36), righteous rebellion (Acts 5:29), and a gravity-defying faith (Rom. 4:18).

Our great God would never give us some pathetic spirit of fear. That's horse crap. That's everything God isn't. Fear has jack-squat to do with biblical faith.

What God did give you as a young warrior was ...

Power. Yes Christian, if God truly invaded your life, then you can say *adios* to being timid, helpless, infirm, impotent, weak, powerless, and incompetent. That garbage gets crucified when Christ moves into your castle and gets replaced with Holy Spirit dynamite (Acts 1:8).

Love. 1 John 4:18 says, "perfect love casts out fear." The revelation of God's great love for us kills timidity before men and any fear of catching a bad cold. God's great love for us should make us holy and confident warriors who do not sweat what the unwashed masses sweat because our covenant-keeping God deeply loves us and powerfully upholds and protects us.

Sound Mind. Yep, you read that correctly. God gives the believer a sound mind. Not a terrified, hopeless, and prone to depression mind, but a sound mind.

Finally, say this next verse out loud and with some testicular fortitude.

"For God hath not given us the spirit of fear; but of power, and of love, and of a sound mind."

Now say it again, louder!

"For God hath not given us the spirit of fear; but of power, and of love, and of a sound mind."

Now say it again so loud that it startles yo' mama and she comes to see if you're ok.

"For God hath not given us the spirit of fear; but of power, and of love, and of a sound mind."

Feels good, eh?

Put that scripture on your TV, laptop, and your smartphone and anytime some satanic fear-addled jackanape tries to offload their phobias on you, read that verse out loud again and then tell whoever is trying to get you to live in dread of men or a bad cold to go pound sand. In Christian love, of course.

Finally, if you still aren't convinced that God doesn't want you to be a terrified Christian doormat to evil men, their rancid ideas, and even Satan himself, then get a load of what Solomon said a true believer will be like …

"The wicked flee when no one is pursuing, but the righteous are bold as a lion." -- Prov. 28:1 (NASB)

Solomon says that boldness is the trait of the righteous and the redeemed and fleeing is the trait of the wicked and the damned.

Here's a little interesting observation: You don't see Jesus fleeing when pursued by religious or political idiots or even Satan himself (Mark 1:13; Matt. 23). Matter of fact, and far from fleeing, Jesus regularly got up in their grill when they went full moron in His presence.

Lionhearted

Same thing with John the Baptist. He wasn't characterized by sporting shriveled testicles and chewing his fingernails. John was bold (Matt. 11:7).

The same goes for the apostles and prophets. They were bold, salty dawgs (Acts 4:13; Acts 4:29).

Oh, and the biblical lovely ladies were not characterized by being, "Oh, Beauregard!" wilting daisies, either. Mary, Hannah, Jael, Ruth, Rahab, Sarah, etc., were bold baby, bold!

Indeed, the biblical protagonists, lauded by Holy Writ, were bold before men and devils (Heb. 11:1-40). They were bold in their risk-taking (Heb. 11:8). They were bold in their love towards the unlovely (1Cor. 1:26-31). They were bold in the faith (Heb. 11:24-27). They were bold in their prayers (Acts 4:29).

They were bold with their sense of humor. Especially Elijah and Paul (1Kings 18:27; 1Cor. 4:8). Even in a culture that wanted to cancel them. Speaking of a sense of humor, comedian John Cleese of Monty Python fame, said, "Humor by its very nature is critical. And if you say there's a 'special' group of folks you can't offend then humor is gone and with humor goes a sense of proportion. And when that vanishes, as far as I'm concerned, you're living in 1984."

The biblical mainstays embodied what Dan. 11:32 says, ... "the people who know their God will be strong and take action."

So, in case you're not getting it: the evil are fear-laden and craven; backward-looking hamsters and the Christlike are B-O-L-D, bold.

Do you need more proof? Check out this verse ...

*"... the cowardly, and unbelieving, and abomina-
ble, and murderers, and sexually immoral per-
sons, and sorcerers, and idolaters, and all liars,
their part will be in the lake that burns with fire
and brimstone, which is the second death."*

– Rev. 21:8 (NASB)

Did you catch whom Christ put first on the list of the
damned? The cowardly. I doubt most sassy youth pastors
would even see cowardice as that big of a deal anymore,
but the Holy Spirit did and does.

People who truly collided with Christ were made in-
stantly bold but now boldness seems to be the gift of the
few young men when it was the common denominator of
all the heroes of the scripture.

Nowadays, Christianity is all about being nice, not
bold.

Would people characterize you as bold?

Solomon says the righteous don't just sport any old
boldness but lion-like boldness. I've had the good fortune
to have been around the big cats in my multiple travels to
the Dark Continent. I've been on three African lion hunts,
and I can tell you with great certainty that they're not for
the faint of heart. The lion I hunted came at full charge to
kill us. Their roar/grunts, as they come for you, will leave
what Kramer on Seinfeld called, "memory burn."

Please Note: There're 3/4 of a million words used in
the scripture and the Holy Spirit inspired Solomon to
compare the Christian with a lion.

Lionhearted

Most Christians just focus on us being little sheep where Solomon says, *au contraire*, the righteous are bold as lions. If we are sheep, we're sheep to God alone. To men and devils, we're dangerous apex holy predators akin to lions.

So, why would Solomon say the Christian is lion-like in their boldness? Well, maybe it's because Jesus is called the Lion of the Tribe of Judah. Rev. 5:5. Hello.

Jesus is not called the Koala Bear of Judah. He's not called the Hello Kitty of Judah. He's not called the Cuddly Monkey of Judah, or the Pronghorn Antelope, or Turtle Dove, or Panda Bear of Judah. He's called the Lion of The Tribe of Judah.

Since we're called to be like Him and it's the Holy Ghost's job to morph us into His image (Rom. 8:29) then, ipso facto, we, too, will exhibit lionlike boldness when we get stuck between a rock and a hard place versus fleeing like a terrified little quail.

Can I get an amen?

---

1. Think of a time you either missed an opportunity or failed to live by your conscience just because you chickened out. Describe how that left you feeling afterward.

2. Think of a time you were in a situation where you were scared stupid, but you refused to let

fear force you to miss out on an opportunity, or back down on your principles. Did that leave a different feeling?

3. How has acting boldly changed your opinion of the thing you were afraid of in the first place? Compare an occasion when you succeeded to when you tried something new but still failed. Did failure feel better than chickening out?

4. Think of something you would like to do but have held back because of fear. What specific positive changes can you make in your own life to face that fear and do it anyway?

Lionhearted

Chapter 11. This Spiritual Discipline Is A Must.

"So I gave my attention to the Lord God to seek Him by prayer and supplications, with fasting, sackcloth and ashes. I prayed to the Lord my God and confessed..."

— Daniel 9:3,4 (NASB)

Young man – are you awake to the fact that having significant influence in an atheistic environment is going to take more than you not watching porn videos, drinking José Cuervo, and smoking crack?

Huh?

These are givens. These are musts.

The young man, in his negation of obviously negative behavioral traits, must also -- like Daniel – take care of his body and his mind in a theological context, thereby developing an understanding of the worldview and cultural biases of the society that God has called him to reach.

Nevertheless, the young Turk, though physically fit, mentally astute, and culturally *au courant*, must realize that this is still not a "might or power" war he's waging with the powers of darkness. He must be mightily empowered by the Spirit of the living God to effect the changes the situation demands.

This is where prayer and personal holiness figure into righting the wrongs of our current crappy culture. An intimate relationship with our Holy God paves the way to a public display of His power over unholy spirits.

You know, we are just plain silly if we think that just because we're hip, smart, and now we're well-groomed, that demons are all of a sudden afraid of us. Those changes are necessary, but they alone will not dislodge demons from environments that have long been their homes.

Come on, Christian – we don't give up our stuff that easily, do we?

So, get it straight: demons aren't going to be evicted from their domains just because we are now a little more savvy than the previous batch of religious indolents. Even with the greatest preparation of brains, body, and interpersonal skills – it's not enough to win this war. This war is one waged in an unseen realm in which true devotion to the Lordship of Christ and fervent, Christ-centered prayer is the only hope for defeating the enemy.

All this talk of Christians influencing society would be incomplete without my making noise about Daniel's personal piety and his devotion to God in prayer. Think about it, young squire: when the enemy was looking for stuff with which to incriminate Daniel, there was only one thing for which they could bust him: he was violating the king's edict by maintaining his prayer time.

Daniel was committed to excellence in all things, including fervent, intercessory prayer. Daniel had to pray.

You and I have to pray because we stand less than a snowball's chance in Miami against the forces of hell if we aren't gathering the Spirit's strength from the secret place of prayer.

We cannot allow the effects of a secular society to make prayer seem as if it is a non-essential ingredient to the reforming of our culture. Changing society in this post-modern techno age is a complicated venture – one that should heighten our sense of commitment to prayer, rather than relegate it to the back burner of our to-do-list.

With the exponential changes that are on top of the Church like Michael Moore on a case of jelly doughnuts, we must retire often with God in prayer in order to re-emerge in the public square with the goods necessary to straighten out a twisted society.

My wife and I had the privilege of spending a good deal of time with the late Leonard Ravenhill, a man whose prayer life and walk with God makes my devotion to Christ seem lame at best. This great prophet of God was an incredible evangelist, a powerful conference speaker, and a prolific author. But the thing that struck me was his prayer life.

Above all things, this was a man who walked with God, and that's the way he would have wanted to be remembered. I heard him pray publicly, and I was privileged to pray with him alone in his study – he was the real deal. I want to let his authority speak regarding the importance of prayer by closing with a passage from one of his best-selling books, Why Revival Tarries (a must-read, by the way).

Why Revival Tarries, first published in 1962, is a powerful exhortation to young adults to wage our current spiritual war in the strength of our Lord and with the power of His might. Here's a few quotes from Ravenhill regarding the primacy of prayer. Enjoy.

No man is greater than his prayer life. The pastor who is not praying is playing; the people who are not praying are straying. The pulpit can be a shop window to display one's talents; the prayer closet allows no showing off.

Poverty-stricken as the Church is today in many things, she is most stricken here, in the place of prayer. We have many organizers, but few agonizers; many players and payers, few prayers; many singers, few clingers; lots of pastors, few wrestlers; many fears, few tears; much fashion, little passion; many interferers, few intercessors; many writers, but few fighters. Failing here, we fail everywhere.

The two prerequisites to successful Christian living are vision and passion, both of which are born and maintained by prayer. The ministry of preaching is opened to few; the ministry of prayer – the highest ministry of all human offices – is open to all. Spiritual adolescents say, "I'll not go tonight, it's only a prayer meeting." It may be that Satan has little cause to fear most preaching. Yet past experiences sting him to rally all his infernal army to fight against God's people praying. Modern Christians know little of binding and loosing, though the onus is on us ... "Whatsoever ye shall bind..." Have you done any of this lately? God is not prodigal with His power; to be much for God, we must be much with God.

Prayer is profoundly simple and simply profound.

Prayer is the simplest form of speech that infant lips can try, yet so sublime that it out-ranges all speech and can exhaust man's vocabulary.

Can any deny that in the modern church set-up the main cause of anxiety is money? Yet that which tries modern churches the most, troubles the New Testament Church the least. Our accent is on paying, and theirs was on praying. When we have paid, the place is taken; when they had prayed, the place was shaken!

In the matter of New Testament, Spirit-inspired, hell-shaking, world-breaking prayer, never has so much been left by so many. For this kind of prayer there is no substitute. We do it – or die!

If you're going to morph from a male young dweeb to an epic Biblical masculine warrior then develop now, young lad, the priority of prayer, in everything you do. Prayer is the first thing, the last thing, and everything that should define you.

Below is the introduction to my best, bestselling book, Psalms of War: Prayers That Literally Kick Ass. Why did I include this chapter? Well, like several of the other topics covered in this book, the subject of imprecatory prayers gets ignored by most yummy youth pastors more than a fat dude avoids sit-ups and broccoli.

What's lost on a lot of people regarding the Psalms is that David must've penned a stack of these when he was a young man. He was anointed by Samuel to replace Saul as an early teen. He smoked Goliath in his late teens, and he was thirty years old when he was formally installed as King over Israel (1 Sam. 17:33; 2 Sam. 5:4). Several Psalms chronicle these raucous times between the ages of eighteen and thirty.

Hence, young squire, as a youth, David was acquainted with, and inspired by The Holy Spirit, to pray down God's judgment upon implacable and impenitent foes who were spot-welded to Satan's malevolent machinations.

Because you too face personal devils, and you too are affected by the ill-will of evil forces in this fallen world, you also should be an adept slinger of these demon-slaying prayer bombs. My prayer is that this little chapter will forever change the way you pray against Satan and his devices. Without further ado here's my introduction to the Psalms of War: Prayers That Literally Kick Ass.

Dear young Christian dude: What do you pray for in a country that's governed by anti-theistic godless idiots who dream about dispensing with God and all things holy, just, and good?

In addition, say that the powers of darkness are on you like stink on a monkey: What do you pray and how do you pray those malevolent forces away, huh?

Also, what do you pray for if the Church you're a part of needs a massive revival because it has blown off seriously following the Rebel from Galilee and has morphed into a PC-addled religious social club?

Finally, what do you pray and say to your cantankerous flesh, that hates God and opposes your noble pursuit of the Son of Man?

One thing's for certain: sappy, now-I-lay-me-down-to-sleep "prayers" ain't gonna cut it when waging war against the aforementioned. Oh, heck no.

Young David faced pure evil, in its multifaceted forms, when he kicked up dust on this terra firma three thousand years ago. He faced foes such as...

- Evil nations that hated God and His people.
- Evil "people of God" who tried to ruin his life and attempted to murder him.
- Evil priests and kings within the House of God

Evil bents from his carnal flesh that tempted him to forsake God and listen to his lower cortex monkey brain that's always in agreement with the Devil.

Yep, David said the enemy had been, "plowing furrows" in his back (Ps. 129) as long as he could remember! But the cool thing about David is he didn't take the enemy's crap laying down. He didn't curl up in the fetal position and wet his teenage Jewish diaper. He fought back. Sometimes he fought back physically. He always, constantly, fought back spiritually via worship and prayer. And not just any kind of "prayer", mind you, but a specific kind of prayer that you don't hear much about anymore in your typical Cheesy Feel-good PC Church even though the Bible is replete with them.

Theologians call these prayers of David, imprecatory prayers, or maledictions. They are prayers to pull out and pray when things get bad. As in real bad. Prayers you use when a nation's getting mucked up by degenerate priests or politicians, or when the enemy is crushing the people of God, or when your personal demons/flesh are out of control.

So, who in the Scripture volleyed these Holy Spirit-inspired invectives toward evil people and places? Well, aside from David, it was guys like Moses, Joshua, Jeremiah, Ezekiel, Paul, and uh ... let's see ... there was someone else. Oh. I remember ... Jesus. Yep, the Prince of Peace prayed and declared some not-so-nice maledictions against a gaggle of corrupt critters who were a hindrance to life and truth on His planet. For instance, sweet and cuddly, seven-pound thirteen-ounce, baby Jesus said the following later on in life ...

> *"Woe to you, scribes and Pharisees, hypocrites!*
> *For you build the tombs of the prophets and*
> *adorn the monuments of the righteous, and say,*
> *'If we had been living in the days of our fathers,*
> *we would not have been partners with them in*
> *shedding the blood of the prophets. 'So you testify*
> *against yourselves, that you are sons of those*
> *who murdered the prophets. Fill up, then, the*
> *measure of the guilt of your fathers. You serpents,*
> *you brood of vipers, how will you escape the sen-*
> *tence of hell?"*

– Matt. 23:29-33 (KJV)

Matter of fact, Christ is credited with saying all the various "Woes (imprecations)" in the Gospels. What's the matter? Did they not tell you that at your youth group? It's true. Google it.

Lionhearted

David, however, at least from a recorded standpoint, was the king of this type of incendiary intercession. This young giant killer slayed more Goliaths in his prayers and songs than he ever did with a rock and slingshot. Oh, and by the way, Jesus said all those imprecations David dealt out were not the mad ramblings of a ticked-off young warrior poet but were actually inspired by the Holy Spirit in Matthew 22:43. Check it out. Also, the apostle Paul echoed the same sentiments when he told Timothy ...

"All Scripture is inspired by God and beneficial for teaching, for rebuke, for correction, for training in righteousness ... " 2 Tim. 3:16 (That "all scripture" entails all the imprecations within Holy Writ. Hello.)

Now, what follows is a sample list, from the book of Psalms, regarding how David rolled in prayer. I bet you haven't heard these read, prayed, or sung in church against our formidable enemies, have you? I didn't think so. It might be time to dust them off and offer 'em up if you're truly concerned about the state of Christ's Church and our nation.

Here's a prayer to pray against evil leaders ...

A lot of people, for many, many serious reasons, are wringing their hands nowadays over the glide path our nation is tooling down thanks to the Marxist morons inside the Beltway.

Yep, at this writing, our current bevy of "leaders" care for that which is holy, just, and good about as much as a badger cares what a prairie dog feels when he's chewing on his carotid artery.

I've personally seen and heard many Christians buy into this hand-wringing over the state of our union, and I have wondered aloud, "Why don't you, dear Christian, cease to sweat these godless leaders and pray that God either convert them or sort them out?"

Here in Psalm 2, David's not sweating a culture's smack talking against God. He's not curled up in the fetal position, sucking his thumb and wetting his pants over their godless and goofy plots to be free of God and cut loose from His law.

Matter of fact, David's reaction is just the opposite of what most doom-n-gloom Christians are boo-hooing about during these days of declension.

Indeed, David states that when rebel-kings start crap-talking God and attempt to dispense with His degrees that God mocks them. Yep, Jehovah's amused at these presumptive idiots who wish to lead a nation without giving God honor by adhering to His way.

And He doesn't just laugh, as you're about to see, He gets ticked off and that's bad news bears for the fools attempting to cast loose from God's gracious moorings.

Ergo, dear Christian, instead of chewing your fingernails down to the numb and buying the fear that saddles the faithless, why don't you pray out loud Psalm 2 that David prayed and penned many moons ago?

Psalm 2:1-12 (TLB)

What fools the nations are to rage against the Lord! How strange that men should try to outwit God! For a summit conference of the nations has been called to plot against the Lord and his

Lionhearted

Messiah, Christ the King. "Come, let us break his chains," they say, "and free ourselves from all this slavery to God."

But God in heaven merely laughs! He is amused by all their puny plans. And then in fierce fury he rebukes them and fills them with fear.

For the Lord declares,"This is the King of my choice, and I have enthroned him in Jerusalem, my holy city."

His chosen one replies, "I will reveal the everlasting purposes of God, for the Lord has said to me, 'You are my Son. This is your Coronation Day. Today I am giving you your glory.'" "Only ask and I will give you all the nations of the world. Rule them with an iron rod; smash them like clay pots!"

O kings and rulers of the earth, listen while there is time. Serve the Lord with reverent fear; rejoice with trembling. Fall down before his Son and kiss his feet before his anger is roused and you perish. I am warning you -- his wrath will soon begin. But oh, the joys of those who put their trust in him!

Here's a prayer David penned that was pointed at a corrupt culture hellbent on following Satan's evil dictates. Check it out...

When one conjures up in their whirring tin brain what it means to be a good "Christian," who has a "personal relationship with Jesus Christ," one imagines ...

1. A nice old man who wears a cardigan, buys MyPillows, lives comfortably, watches Mike Huckabee and says, "God bless you" every time you sneeze.

2. Some elderly lady who clutches her pearls and says, "Oh, my" when she sees a Kim Kardashian butt pic on Watters World via the Fox News Channel.

3. A big, teenaged, frizzy-haired, barefooted girl who dons a We The Kingdom T-Shirt, wears stretch pants, dances with a scarf during worship, and thinks holy water is a real thing.

4. A male hipster dandy who loves skinny jeans, sports a man bag, and quotes more aphorisms during a student Bible study at Starbucks than an over-medicated Joel Osteen would on a three-day Mountain Dew bender.

Suffice it to say, in the American evangelical milieu, being a Christian and having a "close walk with God" is a very comfortable thing, but it was not so for King David.

Being "a man after God's own heart" cost David a pound of flesh.

It meant David was on Satan's Most Wanted list of folks Lucifer would love to obliterate.

Awww. What's the matter?

Did they not tell you that in your "youth group?"

Here's the reality, Ms. Kumbayah: to truly follow The Rebel from Galilee, to live as He lived, and say what He said, in this adulterous and perverted generation will land you in scalding hot water with all that is wicked.

Lionhearted

David had to run for dear life at times from "fierce lions" who wanted to tear him to shreds and David wasn't speaking "spiritually," but literally. They truly wanted him dead because in his live, fire-breathing form, David was a wrecking crane to their idols and their evil machinations.

Psalm 7 shows David in the throes of a serious altercation and how he sang and prayed to God for deliverance. If you're also in such a fray I suggest the following:

1. Lather.

2. Rinse.

3. And repeat what David said here with faith and force and watch God vanquish your foes.

I am depending on you, O Lord my God, to save me from my persecutors. Don't let them pounce upon me as a lion would and maul me and drag me away with no one to rescue me. It would be different, Lord, if I were doing evil things — if I were paying back evil for good or unjustly attacking those I dislike. Then it would be right for you to let my enemies destroy me, crush me to the ground, and trample my life in the dust.

But Lord! Arise in anger against the anger of my enemies. Awake! Demand justice for me, Lord! Gather all peoples before you; sit high above them, judging their sins. But justify me publicly; establish my honor and truth before them all. End all wickedness, O Lord, and bless all who truly worship God; for you, the righteous God, look deep within the hearts of men and examine all their motives and their thoughts. God is

*my shield; he will defend me. He saves those
whose hearts and lives are true and right. God
is a judge who is perfectly fair, and he is angry
with the wicked every day. Unless they repent,
he will sharpen his sword and slay them. He has
bent and strung his bow and fitted it with deadly
arrows made from shafts of fire. The wicked man
conceives an evil plot, labors with its dark de-
tails, and brings to birth his treachery and lies;
let him fall into his own trap May the violence he
plans for others boomerang upon himself; let him
die. Oh, how grateful and thankful I am to the
Lord because he is so good. I will sing praise to
the name of the Lord who is above all lords.*

– Psalm 7:1-17(TLB)

(* Start praying like that instead of the way your neutered youth pastor does. Also, make certain to video people's reactions when you pray in public this awesome psalm.)

For my final example look at how David prayed when the wicked prospered and the righteous suffered...

Have you ever looked at clearly wicked impenitent people and leaders and thought, "Why the heck are they prospering and their wretched schemes succeeding?"

In the meantime in between time, folks that are try-ing to do right, obey God, and influence society with the gracious biblical worldview, are getting kicked by culture like a stuck door at Chuck Norris's house.

Yep, in today's jacked-up world, evil gets the green light and Christianity gets canceled. It seems whacked and highly "unfair" that the aforementioned appears to be the case.

Lionhearted

One would almost think that there is no God, or if there is one, He sure doesn't give one flibbertigibbet about what's going down on this third rock from the sun, because the spawns of Satan seem to be winning and God's people are getting the shiitake mushrooms stomped out of them.

One thing for the Christian to consider before they get all gloomy and begin to make Van Gogh look like a rodeo clown is this: just because God isn't visibly kicking the wicked's backside, doesn't mean an ass-whuppin' is not coming for them.

David dealt with this dilemma in Psalm 10. The wicked during his day plotted against him and Israel. They taunted Jehovah. They defied the people of God. They hunted down the righteous. They scorned God and, seemingly, they were getting away with it. Yep, they were cocksure they would never be held accountable for their hellish actions. But that's where the malicious were wrong. As in, dead wrong.

Look at what David prayed at these hounds from hell. Pay particular attention to verses fifteen and sixteen.

Remember to pray Psalm 10 the next time you begin to think the wicked will get away with their wickedness and the righteous are doomed to be Satan's doormat.

Here's Psalm 10 in The Message Translation.

God, are you avoiding me?
Where are you when I need you?
Full of hot air, the wicked
are hot on the trail of the poor.
Trip them up, tangle them up
in their fine-tuned plots.

Doug Giles

The wicked are windbags,
the swindlers have foul breath.
The wicked snub God,
their noses stuck high in the air.
Their graffiti are scrawled on the walls:
"Catch us if you can!" "God is dead."

They care nothing for what you think;
if you get in their way, they blow you off.
They live (they think) a charmed life:
"We can't go wrong. This is our lucky year!"

They carry a mouthful of spells,
their tongues spit venom like adders.
They hide behind ordinary people,
hen pounce on their victims.

They mark the luckless,
then wait like a hunter in a blind;
When the poor wretch wanders too close,
they stab him in the back.

The hapless fool is kicked to the ground,
the unlucky victim is brutally axed.
He thinks God has dumped him,
he's sure that God is indifferent to his plight.

Time to get up, God—get moving.
The luckless think they're Godforsaken.
They wonder why the wicked scorn God
and get away with it,
Why the wicked are so cocksure
they'll never come up for audit.

But you know all about it—
the contempt, the abuse.
I dare to believe that the luckless
will get lucky someday in you.

Lionhearted

You won't let them down:
orphans won't be orphans forever.

Break the wicked right arms,
break all the evil left arms.
Search and destroy
every sign of crime.
God's grace and order wins;
godlessness loses.

The victim's faint pulse picks up;
the hearts of the hopeless pump red blood
as you put your ear to their lips.
Orphans get parents,
the homeless get homes.
The reign of terror is over,
the rule of the gang lords is ended

— Psalm 10 (MSG)

Lastly, if you purchase Psalms of War: Prayers That Literally Kick Ass, here's how I recommend "reading" that compendium of nuclear prayer bombs ...

1. Go through the table of contents and pick a topic/chapter title that currently concerns you. For instance, if you are sick of sorry, godless, leaders ruining our nation, a great place to start praying would be, Chapter One: A Psalm of War Against Evil Leaders. In addition, say you're beyond beleaguered with watching malevolent Marxists ruin our cities. A great chapter to launch some Dirty Harry prayers at the demons behind that bellicose behavior would be, Chapter Fifteen: A Psalm of War Against Those Who Long For Chaos.

David had many enemies in his prayer crosshairs that he launched these invectives towards. Some physical, some spiritual, and some internal. Anything standing between him accomplishing God's will, on this planet, received a verbal hailstorm from the slingshot-swinging shepherd. I've included 20+ different topics/targets David hit on for you, the reader, to pick and pray in light of what the Lord is leading you to jackhammer in your current local condition.

2. Read them out loud. Yep, read them out loud, at the enemy, and with passion, against the demonic foes of the Church, Family, and State.

    Indeed, don't just half-heartedly read these Imprecatory Psalms aloud. Do it with gusto. Get ticked off and bark 'em at the enemy. These prayers saved David's backside from some gnarly garbage. Give them the proper respect/gravitas they deserve by reading them aloud, with holy emotion, like your butt's in a similar sling as David's was back when he penned them.

3. Get your hipster worship team to stop singing their heretical, sappy, and soulish "praise and worship" songs and put these bad boys back into play. You do know that these Psalms are the Bible's original butt-kicking hymnal, correct? And, I'm assuming, you do also know that Paul, by inspiration of the Holy Spirit, commanded Christians, in Ephesians 5:19, to "(Speak) to one

another in psalms and hymns and spiritual songs, singing and making melody with your hearts to the Lord ..." Did you catch the "psalms" part of that verse? That would include the Psalms of War entailed herein.

4. So, think of this book as not only an *aperçu* of various imprecations to pray against heaven's ubiquitous foes, but also a funky little journal that you can scribble victory notes in after Christ clocks whatever/whomever is battering you and the Church. Imagine praying these prayers and journaling your victories in this book for just a five-year time period! It'll be a veritable legacy book that your kids and grandkids will fight over once you take the big dirt nap. Plus, it'll also encourage them, when you're dead and gone, to also kick butt and take names for that which is holy, just, and good.

5. Finally, this book will do you no good if you do not boldly confess these texts as your promises, and The Church's promises, given to the Body of Christ by God, The Father, to wage war against the powers of darkness. As stated, there are 20+ different imprecatory prayers in my that are aimed at specific demonic attacks. Keep it handy so that when you too undergo Satanic assault, you'll be able scan the table of contents for the perfect prayer against the hordes of hell.

And so, my brothers and sisters, fight the enemies of God and mankind with what the Holy Ghost preserved for all eternity for the Christian to use against Satan's devices namely, the imprecatory prayers. Or what I like to call, The Psalms of War.

Oh, one more thing. Squishy Christians will be quick to say we shouldn't pray these prayers against our enemies or wish ill on our adversaries. First off, I agree. The imprecatory psalms are not curses to be tossed around by aggrieved Christians who want God to waylay everyone who is not like them. Secondly, our battle, predominantly, is not against flesh and blood (Ephesians 6:10-12) but demonic hordes. That said, and it's unfortunate, but demonic forces work through physical sinners to execute their dirty deeds, correct? So, it's a given, in our usage of imprecatory psalms against the clear enemies of God, that there will be human collateral damage of certain people who have decided to follow Satan's will and way versus God's. Therefore, in our volleying of these invectives, our heart should seek the repentance of those, who like Paul sided with the Devil out of ignorance, while leaving room for the wrath of God because He alone knows who are truly the implacable and impenitent and who are in line for a holy butt whuppin' from heaven.

Lionhearted

---

1. Think about the schedule of events at your church. Which events are priorities? Where does prayer rank among them?

2. Imagine a Christian convert from Islam joined your church. (Muslims pray five times a day.) Describe his first impression of your church's spiritual discipline. What about your own prayer life?

3. One of the most common excuses for prayerlessness is "lack of time'" — discuss some of the wasteful things we do with our time that can be squandered opportunities for prayer.

4. If prayer life at your church (and your home) was the example followed by Christians around the world, what would the short-term and long-term view of the Church's future look like?

5. Mary Queen of Scots, a wicked queen who martyred Christians once said, "I fear the prayers of John Knox more than all the assembled armies of Europe." Do you know anyone whose prayer life has that reputation? How would your life change if you believed your own prayer life had that kind of impact?

Chapter 12. I Just Had To Include This Chapter.

(* Author's note. This chapter is from my #1 Amazon bestseller, John The Baptist: A Rude Awakening Precedes A Great Awakening. The reason I included it in this book for young men is because they need it, and I don't know if they've read it yet. Plus, I love writing and preaching about topics today's hipster preachers avoid like Biden does Tucker Carlson. Here you go. Enjoy and you're welcome).

John the Baptist was a 30-year-old wildman. He came from the wilderness and it showed. His clothes were wild. His food selection was wild, and his message was wild. Nothing about John was bland, calm, delicate, mellow, moderate, smooth, soft, tepid, blah, dainty, faint, genial, ho-hum, lukewarm, medium, mollifying, pablum, or beige. John the Baptist was pure, uncut, high voltage, Holy Ghost rock-n-roll.

Yep, young John did not fit in the fashionable religious mode. He was uncultivated. He wasn't a product of human aid or human care. He was not subject to restraint or regulation except by God. He was aggressive in nature and impossible to domesticate. He was unpredictable and temperamental. You couldn't saddle John or milk him. You weren't going to be able to put a ring in John's nostrils unless he wanted you to. Oh, and by the way, God purposely hardwired him like that.

Most young Christian males are the exact opposite of John. They're civilized, cultured, nice, refined, sophisticated, behaved, calm, controllable, delicate, gentle, manageable, orderly, and tame. They're born to be mild, not born to be wild. Matter of fact, here's their favorite song.

Born to Be Mild

(* To be sung to the tune of, Born to Be Wild, by Steppenwolf)

Get my silky blankie
Cry out for my mommy
Looking for some comfort
In whatever comes my way
Yeah, darlin' I won't make it happen
I abuse God's love and grace
Got rid of my guns at once
And fell flat on my face

I like pigs in blankets
Tighty-whitey undies
Passing lots of wind
And gooey banana sundaes

Lionhearted

Yeah, darlin' I won't make it happen
I abuse God's love and grace
Got rid of my guns at once
And fell flat on my face

Like a true subpar child
I was born
Born to be mild
I can't climb so high
I'm not even gonna try

Born to be mild
Born to be mild

Indeed, with most of the budding brethren in the icky recesses of evangelicalism, you can saddle them and ride them. Very few will ever shock you in any holy form or fashion.

John, however, was shocking to The Behaved's sensibilities.

Jesus was a scandalous offense to The Refined's rationale.

That's why they killed them, folks. They committed the crime of being biblical which, by its very nature, disallowed them to fit into some screwy and satanic religious robotic mode of lackluster domesticity.

They were anything but normal.

You know who else was a young wild child? King David was. As a ruddy teenager he killed and decapitated the champion of the Philistines, Goliath (1Sam. 17:48-51). That ain't normal teenage behavior. Aside from that nugget, David also danced in his underwear during a public worship service (2Sam. 6:14). Can you imagine what the pearl-clutchin' evangelicals would say about that? In addition, David cut two hundred foreskins off his enemy's naughty bits as a goof and as a gift for his future father-in-law (1Sam. 18:27). Again, that ain't normal youthful Christian behavior.

Speaking of David.

Out of one hundred and fifty Psalms, or "Palms", as Joe Biden calls them, there are forty "Famous" Psalms according to the experts. Y'know, classics like, "The Lord is my shepherd ..." Psalm 23?

The one we're going to look at in this final chapter didn't make the "famous" cut but I think it deserves a gander because it too is inspired by the Holy Spirit, and it fits in *muy bueno* within the topic of this tornadic tome. Y'all ready? Let's roll.

The Psalm is the ninety-second Psalm and the verse I'm gonna put under the microscope is verse ten. Check it out ...

But You have exalted my horn like that of the wild ox; I have been anointed with fresh oil. – Ps. 92:10 (NASB)

Have you ever heard that verse preached on? You have if you attend the Church that I pastor. But I'm a guessin' if you go to your typical Sacchariferous Christian Fellowship you didn't even know it existed.

Lionhearted

By the way, why are big chunks of the Bible never touched on nowadays in our sassy, easy-breezy, summer-squeezy churches? I'll tell you why. El Diablo wants you in the dark so you don't morph into a major pain in the butt to him. Anyway, I'm derailing. Back to Psalm 92:10.

In Psalm 92:10 David said, " ... You have exalted my horn like that of the wild ox; I have been anointed with fresh oil."

The Message Translation renders it thus, "But you've made me strong as a charging bison ... "

David said God blessed him to be like a "wild bull" ... "a charging wild bull."

Please note that David didn't say, "The Lord has exalted my horn like that of a Tufted Titmouse: I have been anointed with formaldehyde." When God blessed, favored, and aided His special boy David, He made him roll like a wild ox, like a wild bull, like a wild buffalo. Can you feel that? The "wild bull" blessing is what David deemed an "anointing of fresh oil."

I've been fortunate to have hunted four types of wild bovine here in the U.S. and in Africa. I've hunted the American Bison twice. I've hunted free-range Watusi twice. I have hunted Asiatic Water Buffalo twice. I've hunted Africa's Cape Buffalo three times and I've accompanied my buddy Glenn on four of his Cape Buffalo hunts also in Africa. I can tell you this with great certainty: hunting the wild bulls is anything but dull. Especially Cape Buffalo. Cape Buffalo is nobody's fool. They weigh around 1,600-2,000 pounds. They stand about five-and-a-half feet at the shoulder. They're eleven-plus feet long, minus their tail. Yes, Dinky ... they are this thing called big. They're also vicious if wounded or cornered. Their nickname is, "Africa's Black Death." They are a veritable widow-maker. Outdoor writer, the late Robert Ruark, famously said that "The Cape Buffalo looks at you like you owe him money." So, why are the Cape Buffalo so keyed up and deadly? Well, unlike their American cousins, who have no major apex predators pursuing them, the Cape Buffalo are the favorite tablefare for the African lion.

In Africa, there's a group of animals called "The Big Five." This company consists of the lion, the leopard, the rhino, the elephant, and the cape buffalo, and all five of them are deemed, "Africa's Most Dangerous Game." When you hunt them there's a good chance that if you don't do it right you could be pushing up daisies at the end of your safari. Indeed, the wild ox clan has a nasty reputation for making short work of their adversaries. I saw on YouTube the other day some dumb chick in Yellowstone trying to take a selfie with a bison. She thought it was cute how close she was getting to the bull. She was giggling and snapping pics. With each photo, she'd inch closer and closer to the buffalo. What she didn't notice, as she was selecting a filter that would decrease how decrepit she looked on Instagram, the bull started pawing the ground. Yep, the bison had enough of her encroachment on his majestic presence and gored her in the crotch and tossed her like a ragdoll into the top of a big ol' cedar tree.

So, what's my point? Well, it's this my beloved: God wants to bless you with a dangerous wild bull anointing that'll stomp satanic lions, crush demonic strongholds, and annihilate all threats to that which is holy, just, and good.

Lionhearted

For the mild, little safe and tenderfoot Christians that think I'm a bubble-off-level with my musings about God wanting to make you like a wild bull please observe what the Godhead is likened to in this book called "The Bible."

God is not a man, that He would lie,

Nor a son of man, that He would change His mind;

Has He said, and will He not do it?

Or has He spoken, and will He not make it good?

Behold, I have received a command to bless;

When He has blessed, I cannot revoke it.

He has not looked at misfortune in Jacob;

Nor has He seen trouble in Israel;

The Lord his God is with him,

And the joyful shout of a king is among them.

God brings them out of Egypt,

He is for them like the horns of the wild ox.

– Num. 23:19-22 (NASB)

Did you catch that last verse ... "He is for them like the horns of the wild ox." Balaam compared God to a wild ox with wicked death-dealing horns and tremendous, stomp-a-mud-hole-in-your-chest muscle power. Make that a re-frigerator magnet. Check it out. Pharaoh and his doomed armies got the wild ox treatment. They were savagely destroyed in the Red Sea by God in a wild ox fashion. Do you need another example of God being likened to a wild ox? You do? Cool. Here you go ...

God brings him out of Egypt,

He is for him like the horns of the wild ox.

He will devour the nations who are his adversaries,

And will crush their bones ...

– Num. 24:8 (NASB)

Jesus, The Horn of Salvation (Luke 1:69), was a brutal wild ox to the powers of darkness. If you don't believe me then find yourself a modern day soothsayer and ask if he/she can contact Satan for his comments on what Christ did to him and his ilk.

The Apostles, who are also likened to ox (1Cor. 9:9), were a full-on, wild bull, fierce disaster to Satan's devices.

God's true anointing will make you a wild menace to those with wicked machinations, just like our beloved young wildman, John the Baptist.

The Wild Ox anointing will make you ...

- Disobey the Devil.
- Disobey your flesh.
- Disobey bad government.
- Disobey bad religion (Job 39:9-12).

Will you dare to ask God to do for you what He did for David, namely turn you into a holy wild ox for His glory?

"But You have exalted my horn like that of the wild ox; I have been anointed with fresh oil."

– Ps. 92:10 (NASB)

Lionhearted

Or will you remain a mild, pusillanimous, domesticated, junior male Christian milk cow?

The choice is yours.

---

1. If John The Baptist rocked up to your church on a Sunday, would he be invited to speak, or would he get gang-tackled by security?

2. John wasn't afraid to tell powerful and "important" people with the power to destroy his life and even lift his head from his shoulders that they are morally bankrupt and in danger of the judgment of God. How effective has the Church been in discharging that responsibility before God in the modern day?

3. What would change if the church got a dose of the sort of "Wild Ox" boldness mentioned in these passages? What would be different personally? In the church? In the culture? Discuss.

Chapter 13. You Definitely Won't Get Taught This At Youth Group.

My wife and I just watched the new movie (as of July 4th, 2023) called, Sound of Freedom. For those of you who're not hip to the film, Sound of Freedom is a 2023 American action film that stars Jim Caviezel, Mira Sorvino, and Bill Camp. Caviezel plays Tim Ballard, a former government agent who embarks on a mission to rescue children from sex slavery in Colombia. It's a horrifying tale based on a true story that everyone should watch, especially fathers.

Speaking of fathers, one scene from the movie that had me yelling on the inside was the opening act where a dad allowed his kids to be alone with an evil whore who happened to be the front person for Colombia sex slavers.

Yep, the clandestine wicked perverts had a faux company that posed as talent scouts for kids. The stupid dad, deaf to common sense, took his gifted daughter and son to a shady hotel and passed his kids off to Satan's sister who told the feckless father he could return to get them at 7 pm. When he returned, they'd been kidnapped and were on their way to be systematically raped five-plus times per day for the next ten years or so. The demonic things that happened to that little girl and her younger brother would've never occurred if the dad had a well-tuned bull-crap detector.

Young man: Here's something for you to jot down for future use. When you finally reproduce and someone wants to take your precious child for whatever reason and you don't know who the heck they are, and/or you have not thoroughly vetted them, you tell said person to go pound sand. I don't care if it's a frickin' angel, or a teacher, or a pastor, or some sexy Colombian hoochie mama promising you the moon and New York City. Your answer should always and definitively be a big whopping, "No!" Remember this maxim when it comes to trusting other people with your children, "When in doubt, don't." *Capisce?*

Last Father's Day, my daughter sent me a video of a man commenting on an interview he'd seen with a convicted child predator. The interviewer asked the evil Uncle Ernie what sort of characteristics he looked for in a child before he targeted them for kidnapping and rape. The lecherous loser stated that there wasn't a particular trait he looked for in the kid but within the victim's family. If the child had a dad whom the predator deemed a threat, he stayed away. If he saw the dad as disengaged and clueless, a veritable wussified pushover, then he went in for the kill, literally.

Here's another thing you'll never hear in your unmanly youth group: As a man of God and as a father, friend, brother, and uncle you need to be a dangerous threat to all that which is unholy, unjust and not good. Yes, Dinky you need to be a good Christian who's very dangerous to wicked people who seek to harm your loved ones. Make certain that your family knows that you will protect them with all your heart, soul, mind, and strength and with lethal force if need be.

All the aforementioned protective prowess used to be commonplace within the male collective since the dawn of time. Nobody really had to tell young males to cowboy up and play the man. It was modeled by his forebears and was expected of him. However, nowadays it's necessary, especially within the church, to goad males to manhood because Christian males have become evanjellyfish.

For instance ... back in the caveman days, if some cave dude from some other tribe tried to steal a man's brontosaurus ribs, or the wheel he just invented, or his cavewoman, or they tried to harm his snaggle-toothed cave brood, the man under attack would find the nearest pterodactyl bone and commence beating the living crap out of said thievish cave thug. And he would usually beat the moron to death. Like in splat. If he didn't kill the cave thug, he would've definitely left one of those massive, cartoon-sized lumps on their head.

The aforementioned was what was considered normal for men up until the 1960s when the man-haters began the systematic emasculation of the male collective, trying to eradicate any and all semblance of this primal, protective funk from their constituent junk and turn them into a squealy, 21st-century hipster liberal.

Indeed, primitive man understood that to him belongs the responsibility not only to provide for himself and his family, but also the duty of beating the fajitas out of any man or animal that threatened his familia's existence.

The men who had this protective prowess; who did not curl up in the corner of their cave in the fetal position behind a stalagmite, suck their thumbs, and wet their hamster loincloths were the ones who were afforded the right to propagate.

Yep, the primal man did not need to rely on The Cave Police Department, or The Cave National Guard, or Brinks Cave Security Systems.

Oh, heck no. Check it out...

He was the front line of defense. He was there to jack you up. He was the first responder. He was the security system. He was the standing army. He was the cop on duty.

It was his job to protect everyone, everywhere, and at all times, and God help the dufus if they transgressed or trespassed on that which was under his care.

Now, fast forward several million years to now and the ubiquitous prissy males who'd run screaming like... well... a prissy male when serious crud hits the fan in their presence.

No doubt, one of the many sad things about our nation's multitudinous, iPostured, twenty-something males is that a great swath of them don't know how to protect themselves, much less their girlfriends or wives or their poor kids, should things go to hell in a handbasket.

A true dude will beat the bejeezus out of someone who forcibly threatens his family.

A true man will double-tap the center mass of any jackass that seeks to hurt or harm loved ones and innocent people.

I purposely put this chapter in a book for young Christian males because more than likely, you're going to be a dad someday and you're in charge of their spiritual, physical, and mental wellbeing. Very few books for Christian young males exhort them to be protectors of their loved ones. This book shall not be one of those impractical and too spiritual rags. This is Thunderdome, young man. Be the apocalyptic warlord God has called you to be.

---

1. If confused kids today are forming their idea of a dad's role in the family — what picture is culture painting for them? Is the role of husband and dad honorable? Respected? Admired? Or is it ridiculed and denigrated?

2. Since the rise of the welfare state, government has stepped in as a surrogate father and provider. Has that experiment been a success or a failure?

3. What benefits does a dad bring to a family that a man is uniquely equipped to provide? Discuss.

Chapter 14. Here's a Label You Should Long For.

Nicknames can be cool and fun.

This next cultural reference might rifle right over your head if you weren't raised properly on heavy doses of the Seinfeld sitcom. In one episode, Jerry's angry pudgy buddy, George Costanza, started a new job in a jocular work environment with lots of nicknames floating around amongst the workforce. George wanted to be called T-Bone. So, he would always order T-Bones during work lunches. When a workmate heard George order a T-Bone, he ordered one as well and George's boss immediately affixed that nickname to him and not George. Instead of Costanza operating under his desired nickname, T-Bone, George was labeled Koko the Monkey. George was not pleased.

My co-host on our Warrior & Wildman podcast, Rich Witmer, has a buddy named Animal who's part of the

Hells Angels. Suffice it to say, that moniker fits that man perfectly.

Dwayne Johnson's nickname is, The Rock

My buddy Jim nicknamed me, The Tomahawk Preacher, for the unsubtle way I deliver the Word of God. His wife actually carved into my pulpit's vertical post that very nickname. Of all the things I get called on a regular basis by my ubiquitous enemies, both inside and outside of the Church, I like that moniker the most.

Like I said, nicknames can be cool and they can also suck.

Trump's the King of giving sucky nicknames to his opponents that the peeps duly labeled cannot shake. For instance, here's some famous jabs from his first stab at the Oval Office.

- Jeb Bush was labeled "Low-energy Jeb"
- Ted Cruz got stickered with "Lyin' Ted"
- Marco Rubio … "Little Marco"
- Hillary Clinton … "Crooked Hillary"
- Joe Biden … "Sleepy Joe" and "Creepy Joe" and currently in 2023, "Crooked Joe".
- Kim Jong Un … "Little Rocket Man"
- Elizabeth Warren … "Pocahontas". Which was highly offensive, highly identifiable, so for Trump, that's a win-win. He gave the Massachusetts Senator Elizabeth Warren the nickname when she claimed that she had Native American heritage. She is 1/32nd Native American, to be exact.

Lionhearted

My nickname for Alexandria Ocasio Cortez is "Occasional Cortex" because apparently her synapses fire on an infrequent basis.

One of Trump's current primary challengers, Ron DeSantis, has been renamed "Ron DeSanctimonious" by The Donald.

In 3rd grade we had a very mean teacher named Mrs. Beachamp. Guess what we nicknamed her?

Jesus has several glorious and powerful names, but He was also called by demon possessed religious people, a "glutton and a drunk" because He ate and drank with sinners (Matt. 11:19). In Matthew 13:55 the dipsticks in his hometown Nazareth called Him "The carpenter's son" in an attempt to level and neutralize Him. By the way, that little sleight of Christ cost them massive miracles. In Matthew 16, Jesus asked His disciples (my paraphrase) "So ... boys. Who do people say that I am? They told Jesus people were calling Him John the Baptist, Elijah, Jeremiah or one of the prophets". Please note they didn't say Jesus was like Oprah, Mr. Rogers, Jared Leto, Drew Barrymore, or Jimmy Fallon, but a very scary prophet. If you were on the wrong side of God's business, the prophets were not your buddy.

The two brothers Jesus selected, James and John, were nicknamed The Sons of Thunder. Please note that Sons of Sassiness, or Sons of Sweetness, or Sons of Charmin were not the sobriquet that they flew under. They were called by Christ "The Sons of Thunder." What an epic handle to have, eh? It sounds like a Lynyrd Skynyrd cover band or a monster truck racing duo way down in the piney woods of southern Georgia.

Just like Jesus' enemies called Him various names, other saints got stickered also with bynames by their enemies based upon the effects of their ministry. Let's look at three of them, shall we? First up to bat is the Old Testament prophet of renown, Elijah. Look what the wicked beta-male, King Ahab called Elijah.

> *"Elijah answered, "I serve the Lord of heaven's armies. As surely as the Lord lives, I will stand before Ahab today." So Obadiah went to Ahab and told him where Elijah was. Then Ahab went to meet Elijah. When he saw Elijah, he said, "Is it you -- the biggest troublemaker in Israel?"*

> –1Kings 18:15-17 (ICB).

Wow. What badge of honor for God's eternal enemies to call a believer the biggest troublemaker in Israel.

Dear young Christian male: Would you love to have a compromised and corrupt politician and his whore wife view you as trouble on two skinny legs? I would. That's what Elijah got stickered with. Yep, Elijah was the founder and CEO of TroubleMaker Ministries. Can you say, #boom?

So, why was Elijah tagged with the troublemaker moniker? Well, it was based on him being obedient to his Divine calling. God called him to be a troublemaker. Awww … what's the matter? Did your youth pastor not tell you that God calls people to be holy troublemakers? Check it out …

Elijah's calling was to confront corrupt leaders. His work was not to start orphanages. He didn't feed the poor. He didn't have a leprosy outreach. He didn't start an effort to save abused camels. He was not a life coach with a Christian flare. He was not a fashionable and swanky prophet. He didn't seek to be a positive, motivational speaker trying to subtly blend God's message into the corrupt culture by getting a haircut like Ahab, dressing like the backslidden Israelites, and going to formal state dinners. That was not Elijah. His job: scalp corrupt leaders who were leading God's people astray.

Indeed, Elijah's call was not to sing kumbaya. His work was to pronounce judgment on Jezebel and her jacked-up ilk. If Elijah had done anything else, like dog rescues, or marital counseling, or hospital visitations, he would have been in direct disobedience to the call of God. No, Elijah was epic because he stayed focused and did something that all the other prophets were scared to do, namely confront wicked rulers. Would to God that we had some Elijahs doing that today both to the Left and the Right.

Elijah was different because he had an attitude, and this attitude was a threat to all that was evil. He was a hazard to cultural constructs that would keep him and those God loved, dumb and down and beholden to shady leaders. Elijah was not a dutiful and domesticated ecclesiastical cow of the politically and culturally correct constructs. No, my friends. Elijah was a troublemaker for Jehovah.

Next up to bat are two New Testament noteworthies, Paul and Silas. Check it out ...

> *Seeing this movement growing, the unconvinced Jewish people became protective and angry. They found some ruffians hanging out in the marketplaces and convinced them to help start a riot. Soon a mob formed, and the whole city was seething with tension. The mob was going street*

by street, looking for Paul and Silas—who were nowhere to be found. Frustrated, when the mob came to the house of a man named Jason, now known as a believer, they grabbed him and some other believers they found there and dragged them to the city officials. Mob: These people— they're political agitators turning the world up- side down! They've come here to our fine city..."

– Acts 17:5-7 (VOICE)

Paul and Silas, to the enemies of The Gospel, were called, "political agitators." The step-n-fetchits of Roman rule viewed Paul and Silas' ministry as "turning the world upside down." Paul and Silas preached Christ as Lord and not Caesar. Yep, they obeyed God and not some satanic narcissist sporting a toga. Indeed, those under the state's dictates knew Paul and Silas's message was going to ruin their dreams of a conquered populace under the oppression of bad political actors. Compare Paul and Silas to ministers today that kiss political butt and obey anti-theistic edicts doled out by demonic dolts like Little Lord Fauci.

Look how other translations render that verse ...

"These men who have upset the world." (NASB)

"These people who have been disturbing the peace throughout the empire." (CEB)

"These [men] that have set the world in tumult." (DARBY)

"They that set the city in an uproar." (DRB)

"These are they which have subverted the state of the world." (GNV)

"Paul and Silas have turned the rest of the world upside down." (TLB)

"These people are out to destroy the world." (MSG)

Oh, by the way, in case you can't read or haven't read the book of Acts or Paul's epistles because you are either illiterate and/or dilatory, Paul, the apostle, bounced in and out of jail more than Lindsey Lohan did from 2007 through 2013. Indeed, Paul wore county orange more than any other preacher in the entire New Testament. They finally had to chop his noggin off because they couldn't shut him up. Every time they'd try to stifle him, beat him, toss him in the clink thinking that'll dial him down, Paul, like a faithful old Timex watch, took a licking and kept on ticking.

Elijah, Paul, and Silas were named by their enemies as troublemakers. That was their nickname. Indeed, they operated in a glorious *contra mundum* fashion just like their elder Brother, The Lord Jesus Christ.

So, young Christian male, what's your nickname gonna be? Will it be ...

- Wally the Whiner?
- Chris the Complainer?
- Poor You Pauly?
- Gary The Gossip?
- Don The Dipstick?
- Chance The Chicken?
- Time Bandit Bob?
- Slow Sloan?
- Larry the Leech?

- Welfare Willie?
- Scared Scott?
- Horndog Hank?
- Timid Timothy?
- I Need Money Mike?
- Samuel the Slanderer?
- Repulsive Ricky?
- Politically Correct Percy?
- Lazy Lawrence?
- Compliant Chris?
- You're So Vain Vinny?

So … what will it be?

Will it be akin to what James and John, Paul and Silas, and Elijah were called, or will it be more like one of the ignoble names in the aforementioned list?

I report. You decide.

Lionhearted

---

1. If nicknames (like "T-bone") are given to us by others, and not ourselves, what does that tell us about the importance of our actions in building a reputation?

2. Think of someone you knew who got slapped with an embarrassing nickname. Was that reputation easy to shake? Discuss.

3. Biblical heroes had a habit of generating "bad reputations" among society's "important" people, yet many famous church leaders today are afraid to say anything that might rattle the wrong cages. Which groups today would be denouncing Jesus, Elijah, or Paul as bad people? What would they dislike about the biblical heroes? Describe the modern church's relationship with those same groups.

Chapter 15. The Blessed Hard Worker & The Cursed Lazy Man.

Herewith, once again, is some practical advice you'll never get in your "Aren't We All Fabulous?" youth group.

Young squire: If you wish to thrive in a competitive world and move up the ladder of success, versus being a government-handout stooge of the machine, here's how you should operate once you find gainful employment. Which ... uh ... you should as soon as possible. I'm talkin' like at ten to twelve years of age. So... pull out your chartreuse journal and jot down these twenty bullet points.

In the event that you actually do have a job, or wish to one day have one, do the following ...

1. Show up on time (Eph. 5:16).

2. Stay off social media unless your job is social media. Duh (Eph. 6:7-8)

3. Don't call in sick unless your eyes are bleeding (James 1:12).

4. Don't waste your company's money (Luke 15:13).

5. Make your company as much money as possible (Matt. 25:14-30).

6. Always think about how you can better the company (Matt. 25:14-30).

7. Look sharp (Dan. 1:4).

8. Be dependable (1Cor. 4:2).

9. Become known for being "The Can-Do Kid" (2Tim. 2:14-19).

10. Sport a great attitude. Nobody likes a sad clown (Rom. 8:31-39).

11. Become multi-skilled. The more things you can master, the fatter your wallet will become (1Chron. 12:14).

12. Be proactive. If something is jacked up, fix it. Finish what you start (2Tim. 4:7).

13. Crank up your communication skills and try to learn to speak like an adult instead of a homeless crackhead (1Cor. 13:11).

14. Learn how to adapt and be creative with your job (Dan. 1:20).

15. Manage yourself instead of constantly needing a babysitter to make sure you haven't crapped your diaper (1Cor. 9:24-27).

16. Don't be a self-obsessed me-monkey (James 3:16).

17. Don't make ease your chief end (Ezek. 16:49).

18. Embrace sacrifice, sweat, and pain (Prov. 14:23).

19. Treat your employer with respect because, if it weren't for him, you'd be eating government cheese and living in a van down by the river (Lam. 5:12).

20. Understand that there are only two jobs that start on top: And that's grave digging and well digging. Everything else entails starting at the bottom. If you ever want to sit on the throne you must start by cleaning the toilets (Lk. 16:10-12).

Now that I've dispensed with a brief exhortation to smart and hard work allow me, your humble author, to show you what happens to you, young Christian male, if you're lazy.

Here's what the wisest man in the ancient world, Solomon, has to say, by Divine inspiration, about the sluggard, or lazy dude.

ONE: The sluggard is lethargic.

"How long will you lie there, you sluggard?
When will you get up from your sleep? A little
sleep, a little slumber, a little folding of the hands
to rest -- and poverty will come on you like a thief
and scarcity like an armed man."

— Prov. 6:9-11 (NIV)

Did you catch what the lazy sluggard attracts to himself? Poverty and scarcity. Question: Is that what you want for your life? Poverty and scarcity? If you do then stay the laggard who's apathetic, dull, inattentive, indifferent, passive, comatose, inert, lymphatic, moony, nebbishy, and languorous; and you can kiss a sweet life goodbye.

TWO: The sluggard is an excuse-maker.

A sluggard says,

"There's a lion in the road, a fierce lion roaming
the streets!"

— Prov. 26:13 (NIV)

Are you good, young Christian male, at making excuses for why you're unable to fulfill the duties you've been assigned to do? When Solomon penned the aforementioned golden nugget, Israel still held a decent population of lions. So, the ancient sluggard, hiding his ancient sluggardness, brought up the reality of man-eaters being in proximity to his person as an excuse as to why he "can't" work today. Pretty creative, eh? "I can't work because a lion might eat me."

THREE: The sluggard is not self-motivated.

"Go to the ant, O sluggard, Observe her ways
and be wise, Which, having no chief, Officer or

ruler, *Prepares her food in the summer And gathers her provision in the harvest."*

– Prov. 6:6-8 (NIV)

Solomon implies, in Proverbs Six, that the sluggard needs a boss or they won't do jack. I call those types of wussies "wheelbarrow people." They only go as far as you push them and that's it. Do you require constant supervision and prodding? If yes, guess what you are.

FOUR: The sluggard craves.

"The soul of the sluggard craves and gets nothing."

– Prov. 13:4 (NIV)

This is an interesting little ditty about the lazy. The dilatory do have desires. They want to live like a rockstar. They want a nice house, a sweet ride, and the cool vacations, but they won't do anything to righteously attain what they dream about on mama's couch, doing bong hits, while playing video games.

To listen to them blather about what they want and where they would like to be, oftentimes, can be confused with ambition when, in reality, it's a pipe dream.

In my sixty years, I've heard these dreamy clowns talk about who they want to be and where they want to go, but at the end of the day, they sit on their butts and do little to nothing to attain what they crave.

FIVE: The sluggard is arrogant.

"The sluggard is wiser in his own eyes than seven men who can give a discreet answer."

– Prov. 26:16 (NIV)

I love this one. The lazy, who haven't done anything in life, thinks he's smarter than the accomplished.

Please note: The passive person loves... and I mean loves ... to tell themselves, their mother, their three cats, and their clueless wife and/or girlfriend who's paying their bills, that they're the sharpest knife in the drawer. But they're not. They're nothing but a dreamy lot of hot air. They're wise, according to Solomon, only in their eyes and are by their very nature, "fools" whose endgame is a crappy life, followed by destruction (Proverbs 24:30, 34; 6:11).

---

1. In 1905, sociologist Max Weber wrote about the social influence of the "protestant work ethic." In describing a (reformed, Calvinist) subset of Christianity he used words like diligence, discipline, and frugality. If another sociologist wrote a follow-up book about the work ethic in today's American church, what words would be used to describe it? Discuss those answers.

2. Do sermons in your church ever mention work? If yes, do they mention it as a vocation and service to God? (See: Col 3:23,24) Or do they echo the "eat the rich" language of today's secular Marxists?

3. Supposing your church still calls out sin as a bad thing, do they ever mention laziness? Sloth made the seven "deadly sins" list of the early church.

Would today's church have the stones to call out sloth as "wicked"?

4. What connection is there between the sin of sloth and the warning Jesus gave in the parable of the talents? If we are "God's workmanship, created in Christ Jesus to do good works which God prepared in advance for us to do", is it possible that God takes it personally when he looks at His church and sees sloth and lack of holy ambition to accomplish His purposes?

giles
10/9

Chapter 16. The 10 Commandments For A Young Gentleman.

Commandment 1. Don't flaunt your advantages. A gentleman doesn't show off who he is, where he went to school, or his net worth. Yea, the bells and smells, the incense and nonsense afforded by certain advantages (earned or otherwise) don't mean a thing to a gentleman if used as a fig leaf to veil one's utter lack of character and humility.

Let me make it simple for you. Everything that Hollywood idiots, politicians, Instagram influencers, and Televangelists do, do the opposite, and you will be a very pleasant and epic young man not hiding behind daddy's cash, mere talent, a Bose voice processor, or fifteen minutes of fame.

A gentleman understands with all the external trappings of success and achievement he can still be a cultural pain in the butt and a horrible person. Therefore, focus not upon dusting up the transient trappings which dazzle the ubiquitous morons but rather pursue the hidden qualities of internal traits which truly make a young man great, at least in God's eyes. Be known principally for being a good person and not for the stuff you have. Hear me loud and clear: advantages/talent without virtue equals a train wreck.

Commandment 2. Everyone deserves respect until they demonstrate they don't deserve it. The gentleman believes that all people are created in the image of God and should be treated with respect until that person shows they don't deserve it.

That means they don't pout, spit, or drop the F-bomb on their pastors, elders, teachers, or parents.

It's amazing to watch young kids unleash their venom on their parents and others and then walk away smacking their gum. The gentleman respects parents, old people, teachers, police, peers, and opponents -- unless forced, by said person, to do otherwise.

Commandment 3. Titles are important. The gentleman still calls their elders "sir" or "ma'am." I've got friends who have adult children with families of their own who make a very nice living, are close to my age, and still call me "sir." When the gentleman addresses a man, it is always as "Mr. (last name)" and a woman as "Mrs." or "Miss (last name)" until they've been green-lit to use their first name or nickname.

Commandment 4. Everyone else matters before you do. The gentleman is here to serve, not be served. He does weird stuff like what needs to be done versus being some diva who expects everyone to wait on him. He doesn't rush an elevator knocking down granny to get on first. When he comes into a situation, he assesses what others might need, not what he can get from people or places.

Commandment 5. Be helpful. The gentleman sees a need, and if he can assist then he helps. A few years ago, I was out in front of a Publix Supermarket and watched a burglary in progress. The guy ran out of the store, cash in hand, with the clerk and security guards chasing him. It looked fun, so I joined in the chase. The clerk and the guard ran out of juice, and I (along with a cop) got to tackle the culprit. Bottom line with those raised as a gentleman is: Whether it's with tackling a punk or packing a trunk, The gentleman is programmed to H-E-L-P, not hinder.

Commandment 6. Be friendly. A gentleman smiles. He's not sullen or vexed. He's not walking around like a brooding snowflake in a pout pretending to be the next angry supermodel. The gentleman says hello and starts friendly conversations. When I take my buddies hunting with me in the South, they're blown away at how friendly people are. We'll be driving down a Farm to Market Road in the middle of nowhere, meet a truck coming the opposite direction and our host will wave. Invariably, one of my friends then asks, "Who was that?" and our host replies, "I don't know." Then my jaded friends give me a confused look and ask me quietly why he waved. I whisper back, "People down here are friendly ... watch out -- it might rub off on you."

Commandment 7. Use the right words. When asked a question, the gentleman doesn't reply with "Huh?" "What?" or "Yeah." It's "Please," "Thank you" or "Yes or no thank you." They are gentlemen who respectfully ask and don't demand.

Commandment 8. Don't dress like a demon-worshiping, drug-addled, cuckoo bird. Dress sharp, solid, and smart. Send a message to the women out there, by the way you dress, that you're sophisticated, eloquent, and powerful and you're not related to Beavis and Butthead, *capisce*?

Commandment 9. Don't take nude photos of yourself or make sex tapes. Unless you want a life in the porn industry with all the "perks" of drugs, STDs, crime, and a shattered soul, I'd really think twice about what kind of pictures and videos you have floating around on the internet. Lately, we have seen many people have their careers derailed or their image forever sullied by the bad, bad decision of sex tapes. People warn you that the inter-net is forever for a reason. These things can damage you for a long, long, long time.

Commandment 10. Learn some cell phone etiquette, please. First off, put your cell phone on vibrate, alright? There's enough noise pollution in our world without us having to hear your phone blast out hellish music at ear-splitting decibels. Secondly, quit yelling on your phone. Just because you can't hear yourself in your cell phone's earpiece doesn't mean the caller can't hear you. In addition, by speaking softly we won't know how shallow and crazy you really are. Thirdly, if you're going to go nuts on the phone will you walk outside, huh? Fourthly, turn it off during church, okay Lucifer? Fifthly, don't text while we're eating dinner. Try this weird anachronistic thing called "conversing with one another."

_____

1. What stands out in this list as the simplest fix that can make the biggest impact on how others perceive you?

2. Did someone ever destroy the positive first impression you had of them the second they opened their mouth? What mistakes did they make? How will you learn not to be like them?

3. If everyone in your neighborhood, workplace or school was as friendly as you are, would it be somewhere worth living?

4. Why is Rule #2 about respect important? How do you react to people who go out of their way to be respectful to you? What about people who are rude?

Chapter 17. Twenty-Five Red Flags That You're Dating The Wrong Girl.

Here are a couple of maxims to remember when you're contemplating marriage.

Number One: "Marriage is like skydiving ... You don't know if you're screwed until you jump."

Number Two: "Love is blind, and marriage is an eye opener."

The aforementioned are veritable bromides. However, a lot of guesswork regarding what your marriage will look like in the future can be eliminated, to a certain extent, by taking seriously the following twenty-five red flags regarding the girl you're dating who could potentially become your Bridezilla. Ignore them at your peril.

1. She has a high boyfriend body count.

2. She doesn't have a legit, proven and tested, walk with God.

3. She believed everything Fauci and CNN said from 2020 - 2022.

4. She has a horrible relationship with her father.

5. She hates kids.

6. She takes pics of her butt and posts them to Instagram.

7. She's into whatever religion Hollywood's currently surfing.

8. She's a "Boss Babe."

9. She has an "I don't need no man" attitude.

10. She's combative and argumentative.

11. She's a vegan.

12. She's feminist who takes notes while watching The View.

13. She subscribes to several "woke" ideologies.

14. She doesn't cook and she's not into homemaking.

15. She lives for clubbing and partying.

16. She's already nagging you.

17. She criticizes and makes fun of you in public.

18. She controls you with insane demands.

19. She creates drama 24/7/365.

20. She hates your friends.

21. She hates your hobbies.

22. She hates hunting and fishing.

23. She uses her sexuality to manipulate you.

24. She never apologizes when wrong.

25. She is charming in public and a nutjob in private.

_____

1. Solomon had 700 wives and 300 concubines (1 Kings 11:1-3), he also wrote a stack of proverbs warning about getting hitched to a nagging wife. (Proverbs 19:13, 21:9, 21:19, 25:24, and 27:15) Do you suppose that's a lesson he learned the hard way?

2. That same verse about his wives tells you that getting hitched to the wrong woman (or army of women, in his case) deep-sixed his walk with God. If an ill-advised marriage could derail the faith of the wisest man on the planet who had a personal visitation from God, what does that mean for little old you and me?

3. Why do negative attitudes toward homemaking and child-raising show up on this list? Do most men even consider these questions when they're looking for a girl?

4. Why do faith and worldview matter? Do men take these issues seriously in dating? How about Christian men?

5. Discuss examples of people who lived to regret blowing off the warning signs about their girl (or guy's) wildly divergent beliefs.

Lionhearted

Chapter 18. Epic Godly Women Don't Want To Marry A Wuss.

"How do you know what a woman wants?" I can hear the feminists screech at this chapter's title.

Well, truth be told. I know nada about what women want except the fact that there are very few things in life that a flat iron and a bottle of wine can't cure.

Look, I'll own it. I'm not a Woman Whisperer. I'll readily confess that weakness. After thirty-five great years of marriage and raising two gorgeous girls, women are still a lovely mystery to me. And I'm cool with that.

One thing I do know for certain, about Italian women at least, is: if they're hungry do not, under any circumstances, tick them off.

That said, my wife and I have spent the better part of a quarter century ministering to males and females, from all over the world, and one thing I've heard from women of all races, colors, and creeds is ... they hate men who're tinkerpots.

Maybe hate is too strong of a word.

Correction, they like and befriend males who're wussies. They enjoy going shopping with them and sharing gossip and Frappuccinos. However, when it comes to hitching their wagon, spitting out some babies and walking into a room of peeps they're looking to impress, schlepping with a dandy does not even raise a blip on their radar. The sad thing is that women outnumber men, and young men, who would be men, are about as hard to find as 40" markhor is in a West Texas cotton field. Good luck, ladies.

Yep, I feel sorry for the young single women out there.

Sure, it's your day and "the sky's the limit" when it comes to career possibilities and voting and crap. But when it comes to your options of viable single young men to date and eventually marry, the only thing that seems "limitless" on your bleak horizon are popinjays aplenty. Sure, there are tons of young males to choose from, but there's only a smattering of young men.

I blame four things for this massive nutless/gutless glut: 1. Pop culture; 2. Public schools; 3. Sassy branches of Catholicism and Protestantism; 4. Homes without an awesome dad.

Allow me to explain.

Lionhearted

Pop culture has made soft, man-bun-sporting capricious young lads the norm. Public schools have shamed and drugged natural masculine traits from boys. The Church has hard-peddled a soft-focused bearded lady version of Jesus who's more akin to a liberal Austin hippie than the rebellious Christ of the Bible. And women have bought into Hollywood's horse hockey, lock stock and two smokin' barrels, that ladies can raise kids without the input of a masculine man in the house. These four lethal ingredients have created a perfect storm for the proliferation of wussies galore. No wonder lesbianism is all the rage. At least you can exchange clothes and make up. Wait, I take that back. Males now wear make-up. My bad.

Questioning my jaded judgment regarding women and their slim pickins when it comes to dudes, I turned to Facebook, before they banned me for life from my two-million followers, and posed this question to the *chicas*:

"DEAR LADIES: Do you like traditional, old-school, manly men or effeminate males? Your answers are going to go into my book, (with anonymity, of course). If you would, please, give a good, but brief, explanation."

Here's the girls' response:

Angelina -- "I love manly alpha men. Nothing is worse than seeing a liberal man following a femiNasty around Trader Joe's and she's got his balls in her purse."

Laura -- "Gimme extra testosterone for my hairy platter of lumberjack arms and chest."

Jan -- "I like a strong man. That is not afraid to SPEAK up for what is right. Not like the wuss in White House.

There is lots of sexy on a strong Alpha male. That can express himself and what he likes ... if ya know what I mean. Lol. But most important is a God-fearing man. Nothing more strong than a man not afraid to admit he needs God in his life to lead."

Lisa -- "I'll take a pick-up-truck-driving, cigar-smoking, whiskey-drinking, God-fearing, gun-toting, scruffy-faced alpha male any day... bonus points if he can cook what he kills."

Lori -- "I definitely want a manly man who is in tune with himself and with me. He knows his wants and needs and he knows my needs, and we work together to satisfy those needs, wants, in each other."

Mary -- "Traditional. I had the other for 18 years of marriage. After 5 kids (all girls) I wised up and got divorced. He was narcissistic, loved his mommy and was addicted to porn. I now have that traditional old school manly man and sometimes cannot believe the difference -- it's AMAZING!"

Lori -- "I've been there too, still waiting for my traditional man to come along and if he doesn't, I'll stay single. I will NOT settle again!"

Suzanne -- "Manly man please. One who can protect his family, armed if necessary, provide for his family, honor his wife and knows how and when to speak up for what is right. Affection is good, whiny, needy jerks aren't. Belittling others ... not attractive. Using more skin products than I do? Oh, hell no! Suck it up and be a man."

Megan -- "Will any woman admit an attraction to Pajama Boy? I just don't even think women who are with men like that are attracted to them ... they just like the fact that there's someone they can boss around."

Johannah -- "If he takes longer to get ready than I do ... We have a problem! I will also add; if your boyfriend takes more selfies than you do, you both need to see other men."

Clarissa -- "Manly man with pants that fit. I'm also so tired of seeing these so-called men walking around with their man purses. Love my hubby of almost 10 years and all his manly ways including holding the door open for me."

Lana -- "I prefer a strong man (I finally got one!) and love being accepted for who I am, slightly crazy with what hubby calls, 'That Italian gene!' I will make him as happy as I can and look after his health because I prayed so hard for a real man and waited 30 years."

Jessica -- "Manly man if I would have wanted the other I would have been lesbian!"

Jo Ann -- "What good is an effeminate man to a woman except to be a sister she never had!"

Kimberly -- "I can't handle a guy who: doesn't play and/or like sports, who likes cats over dogs, who is a male school teacher and the only sport he likes is bowling, who is afraid of horses, who is a liberal, who cries."

Ashley -- "I prefer and have a real man! A man who works hard and doesn't complain, works through sickness and pain. Believes in physical labor when it comes to disciplining kids, plus a whooping. Likes Cigars and whiskey haha! Wears clothes that fit, and have a beard."

Maria -- "I like a man to be a gentleman and a woman to be ladies."

Staci -- "Totally a manly man. A warrior! I can be tough and was that for almost 40 years. But I wanted someone who loved, honored and protected me to give me the safety to be soft and feminine to the core. I don't have to worry about looking over my shoulder."

Kami -- "I need a real man. Skinny jeans are proven to cut off circulation to their brains. And the only good thing about man buns is that they provide a secret room to hide your tampons. Give me gunpowder and lead any day of the week and twice on Sunday."

Meredith -- "How many expletives am I allowed? LOL!"

From the replies my query garnered it looks like I was right ... again.

Below are thirty-two tale-tell signs that you might be a Man-Child that righteous and rowdy, godly women, will purposefully avoid.

1. You're nicer than Jesus.

2. You're a pouter.

3. You're addicted to fun and allergic to godly duty.

4. You skip church for lame "reasons".

5. You sound like Britney Spears when you talk about serious issues.

6. You're a mama's boy.

Lionhearted

7. You drink from a straw.

8. You take way too many selfies.

9. You are biblically illiterate.

10. You're an angry baby.

11. You're loaded down with debt.

12. You avoid responsibility.

13. You blame others for your sad life.

14. You don't lead courageously.

15. You don't serve others.

16. You're a pornoholic.

17. You smoke weed and eat crap food.

18. You don't exercise regularly.

19. You have a dead-fish handshake.

20. You're not a provider.

21. You're not a protector.

22. You're not a hunter.

23. You're not a hero.

24. You're politically correct.

25. You run from difficult and right decisions.

26. You live on social media.

27. You have no idea what classical literature and music is.

28. You follow the crowd.

29. You're scared to stand up for godly convictions.

30. You don't open doors for women and children.

31. You go Dutch on dates or make the girl pay.

32. You avoid strong men who hold you accountable for your actions.

If that laundry list of ignoble, non-masculine, traits just whupped your backside, don't despair. Just repent and get busy morphing into the man God has hardwired you to be.

---

1. Which of these man-child warning signs do you think are the biggest problems in society today? Why those ones?

2. Do the churches you have experience with have more or fewer of these man-child symptoms than our cruddy culture does? Or do they exhibit different symptoms?

3. Think of the male leaders you look up to and admire. Are they more like the masculine go-getters the girls on this list are drawn to, or are they dewy-eyed mamma's boys?

4. We hear a lot in the news about "incels" raging at the world and committing violent acts. (Incels — "involuntarily celibate", guys who can't get noticed by girls, let alone be marriage material.) Is modern society setting frustrated young men up for failure by telling them it's okay for perpetual children to not grow up and step into the role of being the desirable hombres the ladies this chapter are dying to marry?

5. If a guy wants an old-school traditional wife, what sort of a husband would it take to be to make that kind of life possible for her?

Giles
8/23

Chapter 19. My Final Exhortation.

"Let no one look down on your youthfulness, but rather in speech, conduct, love, faith, and purity, show yourself an example of those who believe."

– 1Timothy 4:12 (NASB)

Dear Young Christian: Do you realize that no matter how neglected and confused you may feel, you are the key, under the discipline of the Holy Spirit, to turn this Titanic of a nation around before it hits the proverbial iceberg?

The prophet Joel said it is the young people who will have the visions that will constructively shape our future (Joel 2:28).

That's you, Dude.

Don't think that God will never use you just because you're young. Throughout Scripture and history, youth have had an incredible influence on our society. The Scripture is replete with examples of God using – and in dramatic fashion – young people.

You know, when most of us think about the type of person God uses, we usually think of some old cat sporting a gray beard, wearing little eyeglasses with a scowl on his face carting around a Bible that's bigger than granny's drawers. We forget that Jesus Himself started His ministry when He was thirty years old and finished at the ripe old age of thirty-three. Check out this short list of young "greats" found in the Scripture and in Church history and let this motivate you to seek God in order for Him to use you in a like manner.

- John the Baptist was a little over the 30-mark when he rocked all of Israel.

- David was a youth when he slew Goliath. When God sought for a man to eternally shut Goliath's pie hole, he found a youth who acted like a man.

- Solomon became king over Israel at an early age, and God gave this young king wisdom that blew away his elders.

- Jeremiah, as a youth, was called as a prophet to the nations – to uproot, destroy, build, and plant them according to the word of God.

- Charles Spurgeon was only nineteen when he began his acclaimed pastorate in England.

- John Calvin, at twenty-seven years of age, wrote his world-reforming Institutes, which has profoundly impacted theological and political thought.

Lionhearted

As Benjamin Disraeli said, "The history of heroes is the history of youth." God has a high view of youth. It's not because they are cute, but because they are spiritually lethal. They are the warriors that God uses to cut a swath through the demonic bondages that hold men captive. Their zeal is proverbial ... and when it is mixed with divine wisdom, they are a severe threat to Satan and his defeated ilk.

All the aforementioned young adults were forces, and he that is destined to be a force will be put on his mettle at an early age.

So, get with it, young man. Quit being a slacker ... get a vision ... get on your face ... and get ready for God to make you the next giant slayer. Ask God to give you the heart of a lion and not the spirit of a chicken.

_____

1. Why are older, more experienced people normally respected more than young bucks? What makes experience valuable?

2. Do some people with experience become a bigger problem than a rookie with no experience? Give some examples.

3. Job's friend Elihu held his tongue until chapter 32 (verses 1-22), where he absolutely lit up Job's "wise" old friends. What made him so bold?

4. What did David's epic poem about God's word (Ps. 119:97-104) tell us about how a young squire can get his head screwed on straight better than "experts" with more degrees than a thermometer?

5. Who are some young warriors in history who absolutely rocked the world in their chosen discipline? It can be art, politics, history, faith, business, science, or any other field.

LIONHEARTED

THE RIGHTEOUS ARE BOLD AS A LION. - PROVERBS 28.

DOUGGILES.ART

Doug Giles

About the Author

Doug earned his Bachelor of Fine Arts degree from Texas Tech University and his certificates in both Theological and Biblical Studies from Knox Theological Seminary (Dr. D. James Kennedy, Chancellor). Giles was fortunate to have Dr. R.C. Sproul as an instructor for several classes.

Doug Giles is the host of The Doug Giles Podcast, the co-founder and co-host of the Warriors & Wildmen Podcast (1M+ downloads) and the man behind ClashDaily.com. In addition to driving ClashDaily.com (300M+ page views), Giles is the author of several #1 Amazon bestsellers. His book Psalms of War: Prayers That Literally Kick Ass (2021) spent 26 weeks at #1 on Amazon. In 2018, Giles was permanently banned from his two-million followers on Facebook.

Doug is also an artist and a filmmaker, and his online gallery can be seen at DougGiles.Art. His first film, Biblical Badasses: A Raw Look at Christianity and Art, is available via DougGiles.Art.

Doug's writings have appeared in several other print and online news sources, including Townhall.com,The Washington Times,The Daily Caller, Fox Nation, Human Events, USA Today,The Wall Street Journal,The Washington Examiner, American Hunter Magazine, and ABC News.

Currently, Giles pastors Liberty Fellowship in Wimberley, Texas (LibertyTX.org).

Doug and his wife Margaret have two daughters, Hannah and Regis. Hannah devastated ACORN with her 2009 nation-shaking undercover videos and she currently stars in the explosive 2018 Tribeca Documentary, Acorn and The Firestorm.

Regis has been featured in Elle, American Hunter, and Variety magazines. Regis is also the author of a powerful book titled, How Not To Be A #Me-Too Victim, But A #WarriorChick.

Regis and Hannah are both black belts in Gracie/Valente Jiu-Jitsu.

Check out Doug's various websites.
DougGiles.Art
DougGiles.org
SafariCigar.com
ClashDaily.com
ClashNews.US
Instagram @TheGilesWay
X (formerly Twitter) @TheArtOfDoug

Doug Giles

Accolades for Giles include …

"Doug Giles brings the heat...as in the exact kind of refining heat the wussified church desperately needs. If you think he is too salty, then bless your heart but stay out of my foxhole because you aren't ready for the battle that has come to the door of the Church. But if you can handle the flames, then get ready to lock shields with Godly warriors called to push back evil at such a time as this. Doug will challenge, inspire, equip, offend, and embolden you...usually all at once and you'll love him for it. Welcome to the fight."

Rick Green, Founder of The Patriot Academy

"There're those men of the cloth that cater to mediocrity. There are those timid preachers that are straight up cowards, tucking their tails to the truth. Then there's those very few warriors. Doug defines that word. He's a 'Spec-Ops guy' in the Kingdom of God. A true David looking for 'five smooth stones.'

LTC (Ret.) Pete Chambers Green Beret,
Special Operations Flight Surgeon

"Doug is a Wild Man."

Matt Crouch, President,
Trinity Broadcasting Network

"There is NO way to describe Doug Giles adequately, so I won't even try. Suffice it to say there is NO ONE like him and I'm grateful for him!"

Eric Metaxas

Lionhearted

"Doug Giles speaks the truth ... he's a societal watchdog ... a funny bastard."

Ted Nugent

"Doug Giles is a good man, and his bambinas are fearless. His girls Hannah and Regis Giles are indefatigable. I admire the Giles clan from afar."

Dennis Miller

"Doug Giles, the perfect dynamite needed to ignite a fire in the belly of every man, woman and child to live like warriors."

Lieutenant Colonel Allen B. West

Speaking Engagements

If you'd like to melt some snowflakes and shore up the brains and cojones on scared and cowardly Christians, then you should book Doug to speak at your next event.

To invite Doug to speak at your forthcoming powwow, log on to DougGiles.org and fill out the invitation request.

Lionhearted

Books by Doug Giles

John The Baptist: A Rude Awakening Precedes A Great Awakening

The Wildman Devotional: A 50 Day Devotional for Men

Dear Christian: Your Fear Is Full of Crap

Psalms of War: Prayers That Literally Kick Ass

The Art of Joe: The Political Brilliance of President Biden

Biblical Badasses: The Women

If Masculinity is 'Toxic,' Call Jesus Radioactive

Would Jesus Vote For Trump?

Rules For Radical Christians: 10 Biblical Disciplines for Influential Believers

Pussification: The Effeminization Of The American Male

Raising Righteous And Rowdy Girls

Raising Boys Feminists Will Hate

Rise, Kill and Eat: A Theology of Hunting From Genesis to Revelation.

If You're Going Through Hell, Keep Going

My Grandpa is a Patriotic Badass

A Coloring Book for College Cry Babies

Sandy Hook Massacre: When Seconds Count, Police Are Minutes Away

The Bulldog Attitude: Get It or ... Get Left Behind

A Time To Clash

10 Habits of Decidedly Defective People: The Successful Loser's Guide to Life

Political Twerps, Cultural Jerks, Church Quirks

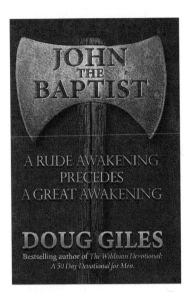

The politically incorrect ministry of John the Baptist was the prelude to the person and work of Jesus Christ. John was the opening act. If we want "Jesus" in our life, home, church and culture then we must embrace ourselves for "John's" abrasive message of repentance. The message that will eternally change you, will first immediately confront you and offend you. The messenger, like John the Baptist, will offend you as well. Those who hunger and thirst after righteousness are cool with both. They don't care if their flesh gets pinched and the message gets pitched by a wild prophet. All they want is God's will to be done, on earth as it is in heaven.

This new book from best-selling author, Doug Giles, is a must-read for any Christian serious about spurning today's worldly culture and getting closer to God.

Lionhearted

Theologians call these specific prayers, from the psalmist David, "imprecatory prayers." They are prayers to pull out and pray when things get bad -- as in real bad. Prayers you use when a nation's getting mucked up by degenerate priests or politicians, or when the enemy is crushing the people of God, or when your flesh/personal demons are out of control.

King David was the king of this type of incendiary intercession. This giant killer slayed more Goliaths in his prayers and songs than he ever did with a rock and slingshot. Oh, and by the way, Jesus said all those imprecations David dealt out were not the mad ramblings of a ticked off warrior poet, but were actually inspired by the Holy Spirit. (See Matthew 22:43.)

Psalms of War: Prayers That Literally Kick Ass is a compendium from the book of Psalms, regarding how David rolled in prayer. I bet you haven't heard these read, prayed or sang in church against our formidable enemies, have you? I didn't think so. It might be time to dust them off and offer 'em up if you're truly concerned about the state of Christ's Church and our nation.

Also included in this book, Psalms of War, are full-color reproductions of the author's original art from his Biblical Badass Series of oil paintings.

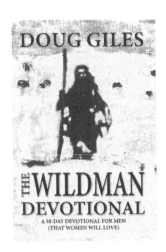

I'm sure some Lysol-disinfected Christian is pearl-clutching over my usage of the word Wildman because they've gotten used to what Satan has sold Christendom namely, a Mild-man. Well, allow me, my fragile friend, to explain what I mean by a biblical Wildman.

Jesus wasn't manageable. He didn't give two flips about what men thought. He wasn't spooked by Satan's threats. He didn't kiss religious or political butt. Jesus was bold, free, and wild before the Father in the epic righteous sense of the word, and you and I should take our cue from the 30-year-old Rebel from Galilee and not castrated Christendom. Can I get a witness?

The Wildman Devotional: A 50 Day Devotional for Men will fuel your inner wildman with solid meat from the scripture. In these 200+ pages you'll feast on the wealth, the walk and the warfare of the Christian, that'll prepare you for maximum usefulness this side of the grave. This book is fire!

Made in the USA
Coppell, TX
28 September 2023

22150466R00116